A COLLECTION OF ESSAYS ON JONATHAN EDWARDS

A COLLECTION OF ESSAYS ON

JONATHAN EDWARDS

EDITED BY MATTHEW V. EVERHARD AND ROBERT L. BOSS

ISBN: 978-0692815076 (pbk)

http://jesociety.org

First Printing, November 2016

Typesetting and design by Robert and Sarah Boss. Cover art adapted from *The Oxbow,* Thomas Cole (1836). Scripture quotations marked (ESV) are from The Holy Bible, English Standard Version® (ESV®), copyright © 2001 by Crossway, a publishing ministry of Good News Publishers. Used by permission. All rights reserved.

Contents

List of Figures

Contributors

Robert Boss (Publisher, Contributor, Typesetting and Design) has his Ph.D. from Southwestern Baptist Theological Seminary, and has served as a pastor in Oklahoma and taught at the seminary and college level at Southwestern Baptist Theological Seminary. He has presented papers at Jonathan Edwards conferences in Northampton, MA and is the author of the monograph *God-Haunted World: The Elemental Theology of Jonathan Edwards*. His long-term project is a visual theology which explores the doctrinal intersections between general and special revelation recognized by Jonathan Edwards and other early Evangelicals. He makes his home in Fort Worth, TX with his wife Stephanie. They have two wonderful daughters—one a student at The Southern Baptist Theological Seminary and the other a recent graduate of Wheaton College. He is the editor of http://jesociety.org, and his personal website is http://robboss.com.

Sarah Boss (Contributor, Design) graduated from Wheaton College in May 2016 with an English major and history minor. Her interest in Jonathan Edwards dates back to early high school, when she first read Edwards's "Images" notebook. She presented a paper at the 2010 Jonathan Edwards conference in Northampton, MA. She also presented a version of the essay printed here at the Midwest Conference on Literature, Language, and Media hosted by the graduate English department at Northern Illinois University in April 2016. Sarah currently teaches part time in Fort Worth, TX, and plans to pursue grad school in Fall 2017, where she hopes to explore her interests in typology and natural theology.

Toby K. Easley (Contributor) holds a D.Min. from Southwestern Baptist Theological Seminary. He was born and raised in Tulsa, Oklahoma. After completing his education, he has taught and preached through every New Testament book at least once and others multiple times in the last twenty-five years. He has a love for New Testament Greek and enjoys analyzing gifted exegetes both past and present. During his doctoral studies, he had the opportunity to research at Yale University's Beinecke Library, where he examined the original manuscripts and sermon outlines of Jonathan Edwards. He has authored numerous research presentations delivered at the Evangelical Theological Society, Evangelical Homiletics Society, and Church meetings relative to the life and works of Edwards. Easley also enjoys road and trail cycling, kayaking, golfing, fishing, and watching sports. In the study and library, he has a passion for research, writing, and publishing. His future goals include authoring additional books, podcasting, and expanding his Feder Ink publishing company. Furthermore, he is praying that during his lifetime the Spirit of God will move in another Transatlantic "Great Awakening," like the one He orchestrated in the eighteenth- century! Toby Easley and his wife Kimberly live in Fort Worth, Texas, and love spending time with their four grown children and four grandchildren, who are all a blessing from the Lord (Psalm 127:1-5)!

Matthew Everhard (Editor, Contributor) is the Senior Pastor of Faith Evangelical Presbyterian Church in Brooksville, Florida. He has been married to his beautiful wife, Kelly, for sixteen years and has three children, Soriah (14), Elijah (12), and Simone (7). Matthew received his undergraduate degree in Bible and Theology from Malone University in Canton Ohio; his Master of Arts in Practical Theology from Ashland Theological Seminary in Ashland, Ohio; and his Doctorate in Ministry from Reformed Theological Seminary in Orlando, Florida. While at RTS, Matthew wrote his dissertation on Jonathan Edwards entitled, "A Theology of Joy: Jonathan Edwards and Joy in the Holy Trinity." He is an ordained pastor in the Evangelical Presbyterian Church (EPC), and the General Editor of EdwardsStudies.com. Matthew is also the author of several books including *Hold Fast the Faith: A Devotional Commentary on the Westminster Confession of 1647* (Reformation Press, 2012).

J.T. Holderman (Contributor) serves as Senior Pastor of Bellevue Presbyterian Church in Gap, PA. He received a Th.M. in Homiletics from Gordon-Conwell Theological Seminary (2013), a M.Div. from Princeton Theological Seminary (2012), and a BA in Theology from Whitworth University (2007). His passions in ministry are preaching and seriously heeding the call to shepherd the flock of God. J.T. became interested in Jonathan Edwards while studying in Princeton, NJ, a one-time home for Edwards and place of his death. His favorite works of Edwards are his written sermons, particularly his sermon "The Excellency of Christ." JT is married to his camp sweetheart Kimberly and they both have one daughter Sophia who is a delight and gift from God. They reside in Lancaster, PA.

David Luke (Contributor) is Director of Postgraduate Studies at the Irish Baptist College (Moira, Co. Down, Northern Ireland) where he teaches Historical Theology and Church History. He previously served as Pastor of Gilnahirk Baptist Church, on the outskirts of Belfast, for almost sixteen years. He is married to Elizabeth and has three children Jill, Emma and Calum.

Zachary A. Hopkins (Contributor) has been Pastor/Teaching Elder of the historic Edgington Evangelical Presbyterian Church since June 2012. Zach was born in Milford, Delaware, and raised in St. Louis, MO. He attended Illinois College (BA Religion and Sociology - Jacksonville, IL) where he was converted as a freshman, and later pursued a call to prepare for ministry at Gordon-Conwell Theological Seminary (M.Div - South Hamilton, MA). His reading and research emphases include the historical theology and ecclesiastical traditions of the English and American Puritans, particularly in the stream of the 17th century Westminster Assembly. His lovely wife, Mackenzie, is the crowing jewel of God's earthly grace to him. Together they enjoy: working out, gardening, and woodworking/DIY projects.

Jonathan S. Marko (Contributor) holds a Ph.D. from Calvin Theological Seminary, and is assistant professor of philosophical and systematic theology at Cornerstone University, Grand Rapids, MI, where he instructs undergraduate and seminary students. His recent research is focused upon Enlightenment philosophers and has resulted in various articles and a forthcoming book comparing the religious epistemologies of John Locke and John Toland. Jonathan is also an elder at his church.

Obbie Tyler Todd (Contributor) is the Associate Pastor of Students at Zoar Baptist Church in Baton Rouge, Louisiana. He holds a Bachelor of Arts in Economics from the University of Kentucky. He also holds a Master of Divinity and Master of Theology from the Southern Baptist Theological Seminary in Louisville, KY. As a doctoral candidate in Theology at New Orleans Baptist Theological Seminary, Obbie is exploring the influence of Jonathan Edwards on the thinking of Baptist Richard Furman. Obbie and his wife Kelly are the parents of twins, Roman Tyler and Ruby June. Obbie is the author of two self-published works: *Mountain Man* (2014) and *Wilderness* (2015).

Christopher Woznicki (Contributor) is a Ph.D. student in Systematic Theology at Fuller Theological Seminary. He received a MA in Theology from Fuller and a BA in Philosophy from UCLA. He recently received a four-year scholarship made possible by the John Templeton Foundation to study the metaphysics of human nature as a part of Fuller's Analytic Theology project. Christopher has published essays on Jonathan Edwards's Trinitarian theology and has several entries in the forthcoming *A Jonathan Edwards Encyclopedia* (Eerdmans, 2016). In addition to his research on theological anthropology he teaches undergraduate courses in Biblical studies, trains pastors in Latin America, and is the college ministry director at a church in Los Angeles. He and his wife just had their first child, a beautiful baby girl.

Introduction

The volume that you now hold in your hands is an experiment. It is also an adventure. Each of the contributors to this collection of essays has provided a unique, thoroughly researched, article pertaining to the life, times, or thought of the Puritan, Jonathan Edwards (1703-1758). As each writer comes from a different background and perspective–some of us are pastors, others are still students, still others professional theologians–we each have something unique to say about Edwards.

As you read this collection, you will notice that some of the essays are of a more devotional nature (Sarah Boss; J.T. Holderman), while others are entirely technical (Jon Marko; Toby Easley; David Luke). Yet tying all of these various perspectives together is the towering figure from the eighteenth century in the person of Jonathan Edwards himself.

The Puritan preacher from Northampton, of course, is interesting enough to fill many such volumes. For this reason, the style and content of each piece that follows varies. Some articles are quite short, and others much longer! Some will focus on pastoral, theological, or ministerial aspects of Edwards's thought (for instance, my own articles). Others will consider Edwards's time and influence from a wider angle. Still others will consider his impact historically as well as his abiding importance today (Obbie Tyler Todd; Chris Woznicki; Zach Hopkins).

I should tell you a bit about how this volume came to be.

Several months ago, I was corresponding with a few other Edwards scholars, and we were sharing the various angles and nuances from which we were each studying Edwards. One scholar, Dr. Rob Boss, the purveyor of the JE Society website, and author of an excellent book about Edwards's typology, suggested that we collaborate. After a few more such pleasant conversations, we determined to invite a wide range of contributors to submit an original piece on Edwards, which we could jointly publish as a collection of essays. Thus, our broad spectrum of contributors are so beautifully varied!

Our hope is that this volume will not be alone, but will be followed by other publishing ventures that focus on Edwards, while simultaneously providing a voice to the rising generation of Edwards scholars. We are all gaining so much from those who have come before us. Men like Ken Minkema and Oliver Crisp have done much for our own up-and-coming class of Edwards scholars. Partially, we meant this book to be a tribute to our own teachers and mentors, as much as it was an invitation to newer thinkers to put pen to paper.

Personally, I think it is thrilling to give younger writers a place and a voice at the table. This is why I rejoice to be able to bring some fresh faces (brilliant too, I might add!) into the arena of Edwards discussion and scholarship.

Finally, I would also do well to give some words of special thanks. All of our contributors are amazing people, and such fun to work with. My friend Susan Jackson did some incredible work for our writers by reviewing their drafts grammatically and structurally, and assisting me with preparing these essays for publication. Dr. Rob Boss and the JE Society provided wonderful typesetting and formatting for this handsome volume. Of course, as the General Editor of this collection, any outstanding faults and imperfections that make it through the publishing process will no doubt rest upon my own shoulders; and for this I humbly beg the reader's forgiveness.

Matthew Everhard

Jonathan Edwards: A Biographical Sketch

J.T. HOLDERMAN

D. Martyn Lloyd-Jones once said, "I am tempted, perhaps foolish, to compare the Puritans to the Alps, Luther and Calvin to the Himalayas, and Jonathan Edwards to Mount Everest."[1] So too, "Reverend Princeton theologian Benjamin B. Warfield agrees, asserting that Edwards 'stands out as the one figure of real greatness in the intellectual life of colonial America.' "[2] R.C. Sproul writes that Edwards's *Freedom of the Will* "is the most important theological work ever published in America."[3] He was a mammoth figure in the history of theology and the history of America. He is worthy of our consideration as a leader to remember.

Jonathan Edwards was born October 5, 1703, in Windsor, Connecticut. He had ten sisters and not a single brother. He could probably knit and crochet with the best. He was of superior intellect and, at twelve years of age, his father sent him to Yale where Edwards flourished. He was a thinker, appearing to have always had his pen in hand taking notes as he read. At the age of 16, he graduated from Yale as valedictorian and gave the graduation address in Latin. He was brilliant.

At 17 years of age, while studying for a master's degree at Yale, Edwards found himself converted to Jesus Christ after studying 1 Timothy 1:17, *To the King of ages, immortal, invisible, the only god, be honor and glory forever and ever.* Edwards wrote that "There came into my soul, and was as it were diffused through it, a sense of the glory of the Divine Being; a new sense, quite different from anything I ever experienced before."[4] Edward's love and unrelenting aim to glorify God began here as he grasped the "glory of the Divine." It is perhaps the glory of God that sums up Edward's pursuit in life better than any other end.

At 19 years of age, Edwards took his first call as interim pastor to Scotch Presbyterian Church in New York with his utmost aim of declaring the glory of God in all that he did. He returned to Yale after the interim period as an instructor and there met his soon to be wife, Sarah Pierrepont. She was, according to Edward's own hand, "...of a wonderful sweetness, calmness and universal benevolence of mind...and seems to be always full of joy and pleasure."[5] Over the

[1] Lloyd-Jones 1987, p. 355

[2] Lawson 2008, p. 4

[3] Sproul 1996, bookjacket

[4] As quoted in Murray 1987, pp. 35-36

[5] *WJE* 10:279

Fig. 1: Jonathan Edwards (1855), by R. Babson & J. Andrews

next 23 years of their lives together they had eight daughters and three sons.

In 1726, God called Edwards to assist his grandfather, Solomon Stoddard, a famous preacher in his own right, in ministering to the esteemed Church of Northampton, Massachusetts. Stoddard passed away three years later and Edwards succeeded Stoddard as sole minister. His primary task as a pastor was the ardent study of the Scriptures; He said: "Be assiduous in reading the Holy Scriptures. This is the fountain whence all knowledge in divinity must be derived. Therefore let not this treasure lie by you neglected."[6] To Edwards, the greatest impact and good he could do as a pastor was to study well the Word of God and communicate its truth in all that he did, be that preaching, conversation, or through his prolific writing.

[6] *WJEO* 54

Edwards's unrelenting resolve to live his life for the glory of God took flame under the Spirit's fanning and played a prominent role in the Great Awakening. New England blossomed under the Calvinistic preaching of Edwards (along with George Whitefield). During the revival, it was estimated that "out of a population of 300,000, between 25,000 and 50,000 new members were added to the churches."[7] During the apex of the awakening, Edwards preached what has come to be known as his most famous sermon (and subsequently the most famous sermon in American history), "Sinners in the Hands of an Angry God." God had so orchestrated Edwards's preaching to fan into flame the faith and lives of believers in New England. At the center of this awakening rested Edwards's love for the supremacy of God.

[7] Kuiper 1951, p. 420

Fig. 2: George Whitefield (1714–70)

In 1757, after 23 years as pastor of Northampton, and years spent writing and thinking in Stockbridge, Massachusetts, Edwards was called by Princeton College to assume the role of the college's President. It was a crowning achievement to be extended this invitation. He took it, although he initially resisted the opportunity due to his ailing health and grand writing dreams. However, on March 22, 1758, after only assuming the position of President of Princeton a month earlier, Edwards passed away after complications that arose from a smallpox inoculation.

Edwards is an example to us as a man who was fixed upon God as his ultimate end in all of life. Due to his writings that have been well preserved, we have a good corpus from which to "remember" his faith and imitate it in our lives. Here are three great things that Edwards strived for in the exercise of his faith that would benefit us to recall:

We Were Created to Glorify God

Uppermost in all of Edwards's life was the great Reformed pillar of *Soli Deo Gloria*. Edwards's faith spurred his understanding of his purpose as one created to magnify and extol God's glory in all that he put his hand to. While he was a sinner and couldn't accomplish this perfectly, it was nonetheless chief in his mind for what was the primary end in his life, God's glory. For as Edwards says:

> Thus we see that the great and last end of God's works which is so variously expressed in Scripture, is indeed but *one;* and this *one* end is most properly and comprehensively called, 'the glory of God.'[8]

[8] *WJE* 8:530

It would be very difficult to overemphasize Edwards's love for God's glory and majesty. His life was set as a flint to kindling for setting ablaze the glory of God in the minds and hearts of those he came in contact with. Simply put, Edwards's drive was not fame, success, money, comfort, family. It was, instead, that people might see the Lord in His glory. Perhaps James Montgomery Boice puts it best: "Common to all of Edwards's theology and piety was a passion for God's glory …Edwards carefully and logically defended the position that God's ultimate purpose is to glorify himself in all his works."[9]

[9] Boice and Ryken 2002, p. 49

With God's glory in mind, Edwards would commend to us a powerful way of viewing it, juxtaposing it alongside our sinful nature. The beauty of God's glory is seen to be more beautiful the more we recognize the ugliness of our sin. In other words, the more depraved we are, the more we have to glory in our God and His gracious stance towards us in Jesus Christ:

> God hath made man's emptiness and misery, his low, lost and ruined state into which he is sunk by the fall, an occasion of the greater advancement of his own glory…as there is now a much more universal and apparent dependence of man on God.[10]

[10] Kimnach et al. 1999, p. 79

Edwards's resolve for God's glory is a wonderful witness to us of our purpose in life. May we imitate his resolve and find our faith ablaze in light of God's glorious Self.

We Were Created To Delight in God

To many, the Christian faith looks like a joyless prison. It is a religion of prohibition: you can't get drunk, you can't sleep around, you can't lie on your taxes. Many in the world see Christianity as a set of rules that restrict the individual and take all "fun" out of life. Edwards, however, would encourage us that it's exactly the opposite for the Christian. He roots the fundamental core of Christianity in relation to an individual's happiness, freedom, and joy, not in a prison of constraint and obedience. Christianity does not kill delight; it, instead, magnifies it and puts it in its proper place. Edwards says it this way:

God is glorified not only by His glory's being seen, but by its being rejoiced in. When those that see it delight in it, God is more glorified than if they only see it.[11]

[11] As quoted in Piper 1998, p. 79

Edwards contends that when we live in our created purpose in Christ, namely to glorify God, we do so successfully only when we do so out of delight. Because the Christian, if he truly grasps the saving faith that is given freely by God's grace in Jesus, realizes that he has found the most joyful pursuit in all of life, giving glory to his creator who has created new life in him. And God is the most joyful pursuit because "He is [our] highest good ... the sum of all that good which Christ purchased. God is the inheritance of the saints; he is the portion of their souls."[12] Edwards knew for the Christian that delight in God was as natural as satiating hunger with food, "True saints have their minds, in the first place, inexpressibly pleased and delighted with the sweet ideas of the glorious and amiable nature of the things of God."[13] Delighting in God is natural for the Christian.

[12] Kimnach et al. 1999, p. 74

[13] WJE 2:250

And so, from Edwards we can learn that we are to delight in our God, in His goodness towards us. When indeed we do see the ugliness of our sinful rebellion in light of God's mercy and grace that He freely gives, we should be brought to a state of utter thankfulness. We should wonder why God would love a sinner such as us to the point of going to the cross to redeem us. When our sin is placed alongside God's mercy and grace, we delight in God's goodness, and in so doing bring glory to God. Edwards knew we were created to savor and delight in our Creator and Redeemer and he would plead with us to do so.

We Were Created to Pursue God

Edwards was a man of great resolve. He was a man who put his mind to a task and did not waver. If he lived today, Facebook and Twitter would not have been a distraction during his work. He was intensely driven in all that he did. John Piper says of Edwards, "There was a single-mindedness that governed his life and enabled him to accomplish amazing things."[14] His constitution was set this way in particular because he understood the seriousness of what he was called to do, namely to redirect hearts and minds to God's glory. We can't escape God's glory with Edwards. With his serious resolve Edwards found himself in a relentless pursuit of God.

[14] Piper 1998, p. 52

His relentless drive to be Godward in all he did is well attested to in his many *Resolutions* that he wrote to steel himself with regards to how he aimed to live his life, namely for God's glory.[15] With 1 Corinthians 10:31 as his guide, *whatever you do, do it all for the glory of God,* Edwards produced a list of 70 resolutions to guide his life and pursuit of God's glory. These are no mere New Year's Resolutions like we might initially

[15] WJE 16:753–59

think. His earnest desire to pursue his delight and devotion to God manifested itself in many intentional aims for his life. May these few resolutions be an encouragement to you to imitate his faith, a faith that calls us to be enamored in our pursuit of knowing and displaying God's glory in our lives, a pursuit that leads to our joy and delight in God.

> 1. Resolved, that I will do whatsoever I think to be most to the glory of God, and my own good, profit, and pleasure, in the whole of my duration...

> 4. Resolved, never to do any manner of thing, whether in soul or body, less or more, but what tends to the glory of God...

> 6. Resolved, to live with all my might, while I do live.

> 7. Resolved, never to do any thing, which I should be afraid to do if it were the last hour of my life.

> 28. Resolved, to study the Scriptures so steadily, constantly, and frequently, as that I may find and plainly perceive, myself to grow in the knowledge of the same.

> 52. I frequently hear persons in old age say how they would live, if they were to live their lives over again: resolved, that I will live just so as I can think I shall wish I had done, supposing I live to old age.

> 67. Resolved, after afflictions, to inquire, what I am the better for them, what good I have got by them, and what I might have got by them.

Edwards was a man of resolve. May we learn from the greatest American theologian and imitate his faith. His was a faith that knew its sole resolve was to pursue God's glory in his life. May we resolve, by faith, to be so fixed on God in our lives so as to display His glory as our all-consuming satisfaction and delight and drive in all that we do as Edwards so clearly demonstrated in his life and death.

Edwards and Thoreau:
Typologies of Lakes

SARAH BOSS

Herman Melville remarks in *Moby-Dick,* "Yes, as everyone knows, meditation and water are wedded for ever."[1] Whether "everyone" knows this is not certain, but two other stalwarts of American thought surely did. Jonathan Edwards and Henry David Thoreau both give water serious meditation—Thoreau perhaps more famously in Walden, while Edwards's meditations on water appear throughout his work, but especially in his journal "Images of Divine Things." Although these two men operate within contrasting schemata—Edwards extending the Puritan tradition of emblems and typology into the realm of nature, and Thoreau adhering to the transcendentalist veneration of nature— they meditate on the exact same image of water. In the chapter of *Walden,* "The Ponds," and in "Image" no. 117 of "Images of Divine Things," Thoreau and Edwards both reflect on the image of a pond which is so clear and still that it reflects the sky in its surface. A close reading of Edwards's and Thoreau's accounts of still water reveals a striking similarity in these two writers' *techne.* They create parallel discourses on water, as they assert the water's significance, describe the water vividly, then finally imagine a descent into the water. However, despite these similarities, they arrive at contrasting conclusions. For Edwards, such a lake is "death" and "darkness itself," but for Thoreau, Walden is "remarkable" for its "purity." Ultimately, their contrasting conclusions reveal irreconcilable differences in methodology, resulting in two distinct modes of typology.

Edwards begins "Image" no. 117 with an explicit statement of his typology. Traditionally, typology is the reading and understanding of Old Testament "types" in light of their New Testament "antitypes" or fulfillment, but Edwards extends his reading beyond Scripture to include nature. In this image, he frames his typological reading as a poignant thesis. He writes, "The water, as I have observed elsewhere, is a type of sin or the corruption of man, and of the state of misery that

Fig. 3: Henry David Thoreau (1817–62)

[1] Melville 2002, p. 19

[2] *WJE* 11:94

is the consequence of it."[2] By asserting that water "is a type of" sin and corruption, Edwards accomplishes two things: First, he announces that he will interpret a universal image of a body of water, rather than one specific lake or pond, thus universalizing his forthcoming interpretation. Second, he establishes a strong sense of typology by using a being verb rather than simile or metaphorical language, thus clearly equating the "type" with his reading of it. Edwards's strong, direct language and the placement of a clear thesis at the beginning of his entry strengthen his typological interpretation. Edwards moves to demonstrate his thesis through a description of the water's "flattering appearance." He writes, "How smooth and harmless does the water oftentimes appear, and as if it had paradise and heaven in its bosom. Thus when we stand on the banks of a lake or river, how flattering and pleasing does it oftentimes appear, as though under were pleasant and delightful groves and bowers, or even heaven itself in its clearness..."[3] Here Edwards uses vivid imagery of heaven reflected on a lake's surface to illustrate the comparison between such water and deceptive sin. His use of "we" invites the reader to join him in a communal memory and empathize with his rendering of the image, drawing her to the water's beatific appearance. The clarity of Edwards's thesis, combined with his succinct but vivid imagery, creates a firm foundation for his interpretation.

[3] *WJE* 11:94

Thoreau's thesis is more nuanced. He begins his first account of Walden Pond, "The scenery of Walden is on a humble scale, and, though very beautiful, does not approach to grandeur, nor can it much concern one who has not long frequented it or lived by its shore; yet this pond is so remarkable for its depth and purity as to merit a particular description."[4] Here Thoreau may seem almost self-deprecating, but buried in this unassuming start is a quiet thesis, which he will aim to demonstrate through his description of the pond. By stating that Walden is humble and without grandeur, then claiming that it is nevertheless "remarkable," Thoreau elevates Walden above other landscapes or bodies of water that may seem more grand. He differs from Edwards in that he does not propose to address a universal image of water, but rather one specific body and its special attributes. The characteristic that merits such elevation is Walden's "purity." Thoreau will spend the body of this description of Walden discussing its color. He describes Walden's color as being "blue at one time and green at another," and recalls, "I have discerned a matchless and indescribable blue light, such as watered or changeable silks and sword blades suggest, more cerulean than the sky itself."[5] Such is the purity and beauty of Walden that all other ponds are merely "yellowish" and "but muddy by comparison." The contrast between Walden's purity and other ponds' muddiness lends Walden a special quality, as if it possessed some inherent goodness.

[4] Thoreau 2006, p. 128

[5] Thoreau 2006, p. 128–29

Furthermore, like Edwards, Thoreau notes the reflection of the sky on the water's surface. He writes of Walden: "Lying between the earth and the heavens, it partakes of the color of both," and he notes again times when "the surface of the waves may reflect the sky."[6] Noting Walden's purity enables Thoreau to argue that it "partakes" of both heaven and earth, essentially acting as a mediator between the two—physically, but also symbolically. Moreover, by claiming that Walden's color is "more cerulean than the sky itself," Thoreau elevates the water above heaven. Giving Walden this heavenly quality suggests a symbolic essence of the water and prompts the reader to consider the double meaning of "purity"—physically, in terms of color, but also metaphysically, through ontological value.

Although Edwards and Thoreau have thus differed slightly in form, with Thoreau creating a more nuanced thesis, the real deviation comes after their parallel descent into the water. Edwards, after describing the "paradise and heaven" depicted on the water's surface, sharply reasserts his thesis: "But indeed, it is all a cheat."[7] He subsequently envisions a scenario in which he and the reader are successfully tempted to enter into the water: "If we should descend into it, instead of finding pleasant, delightful groves and a garden of pleasure, and heaven in its clearness, we should meet with nothing but death, a land of darkness, or darkness itself."[8] In Edwards's account of a descent into the water, he emphasises the "cheat" of the image and the stark contrast between appearance and reality. The "garden of pleasure," with its Edenic connotations, is exposed as "a land of darkness." Edwards's tone and use of the hypothetical "if" demarcate this passage as an urgent warning, rather than mere naturalistic description. Whoever descends into the water, in Edwards's account, undergoes a sort of transformation; however, in this transformation the water does not purify but kills.

Thoreau's account, though containing a parallel descent into the water, could not be more different from Edwards's. Expanding on his thesis of Walden's purity, Thoreau writes, "This water is of such crystalline purity that the body of the bather appears of an alabaster whiteness, still more unnatural, which, as the limbs are magnified and distorted withal, produces a monstrous effect, making fit studies for a Michael Angelo."[9] The purity and unearthliness that appeared in the water are shown to be true by a descent into it. Thoreau's bather is also transformed—not by death but by apotheosis—as she becomes immortalized as a living work of art. At the end of this passage on Walden, Thoreau finally asserts his typological reading of the pond, as water that is not only pure in its appearance but which also purifies those who experience it. Such a transformation, in which the bather transcends her own humanity, reveals the duality of meaning in Thoreau's "purity." The pure appearance of Walden—unlike any other

[6] Thoreau 2006, p. 128

[7] WJE 11:94

[8] WJE 11:94–95

[9] Thoreau 2006, p. 129

water—transfigures whoever is willing to embrace it. So, too, does an intellectual embrace of Walden—seeing it for its true "remarkable" self—enable a purification and transcendence of the mind.

Ultimately, Edwards and Thoreau were able to arrive at these contrasting interpretations because of their differing methodologies. In composing these accounts, they drew from different sources and operated out of clashing ideological frameworks. Edwards's source for his typology was vast, as he cited Scripture to confirm his interpretations of nature. In "Image" no. 156 Edwards writes,

> The Book of Scripture is the interpreter of the book of nature two ways: [first] by declaring to us those spiritual mysteries that are indeed signified or typified in the constitution of the natural world; and secondly, in actually making application of the signs and types in the book of nature as representations of those spiritual mysteries in many instances.[10]

[10] *WJE* 11:106

In this entry, Edwards clearly presents Scripture as the foundational interpretative tool through which nature should be read. In "Image" no. 117 in particular, Edwards connects his reading of lakes back to Scripture. He concludes the entry with a footnote: "Prov. 5:3–6," which is a reference to a "forbidden woman" whose appearance is pleasing and flattering-like Edwards's lake—but whose "feet go down to death." Although his naturalistic observations and typological logic are sound in themselves, Edwards presents Scripture as his final evidence. Although these verses do not mention water, they use metaphor to demonstrate the same type of sin, corruption, and consequent misery as Edwards's thesis, thus communicating the same absolute truth. Additionally, "Images of Divine Things" displays an extensive consideration of water, as Edwards examines water in its vicissitudes and uses biblical references to interpret it. These include: "Image" no. 15, flowing rivers are the effusions of the Spirit; "Image" no. 27, the stormy sea is the wrath of God; "Image" no. 77, the confluence of rivers flowing in various directions into the ocean is divine providence; "Image" no. 155, spring streams that rise then dry up again represent hypocrites; and so on. This wide consideration of water allows Edwards to make an informed, nuanced interpretation of a specific type of water, supported both by biblical sources and comparison with other naturalistic observations.

By contrast, although Thoreau cites writers, philosophers, and scientists throughout Walden, he does not explicitly draw on extra-textual sources when developing his account of the pond. Instead, he relies on his own empirical observations and poetic insight. He, too, is painstaking in his interpretation, as he seems to describe Walden exhaustively, even through seasonal changes. Yet he narrows his observations to focus on one specific pond—he can cannot come to a universal conclusion about ponds or lakes nor does he attempt to. He notes himself that his interpretation of Walden would be lost on anyone who has not been there. Moreover, in a tone of righteous indignation, Thoreau concludes "The Ponds": "Talk of heaven! Ye disgrace earth."[11] This spirited conclusion reaffirms Thoreau's own elevation of earth over heaven and his emphasis on a nature-centric typology, revealing the heart of difference between Edwards and himself. Edwards's typology is a conduit for looking outward and obtaining knowledge about the God who exists above the natural world, while Thoreau's typology flows from an inward sight, like Emerson's transparent eyeball, by which one is able to see the god within.

[11] Thoreau 2006, p. 144

Despite various similarities and differences in their typology, Edwards and Thoreau both acknowledge the spiritual significance of nature and its intentional symbolism. In "Image" no. 57, Edwards writes,

> 'Tis very fit and becoming of God, who is infinitely wise, so to order things that there should be a voice of his in his works instructing those that behold them, and pointing forth and showing divine mysteries and things more immediately appertaining to himself and his spiritual kingdom. The works of God are but a kind of voice or language of God, to instruct intelligent beings in things pertaining to himself.[12]

[12] *WJE* 11:67

For Edwards, a typological truth embedded in nature is in accord with God's own methods of instruction. To extend typology from the Book of Scripture to the Book of Nature only enhances God's communication with humankind. Likewise, although Thoreau does not adhere to orthodox Christianity and traditional typology, he also posits an intentional, truth-laden symbolism inherent in nature. Concerning Walden, he writes, "I am thankful that this pond was made deep and pure for a symbol."[13] This language of intentional symbolism—being "made for" a symbol—communicates a natural typology similar to Edwards's. Ultimately, Edwards's and Thoreau's differing typologies of lakes both point to the universal symbolism of nature and its epiphanic, not just aesthetic, value.

[13] Thoreau 2006, p. 206

Jonathan Edwards: Calvinistic Homeboy or Reformed Eccentric?

MATTHEW EVERHARD

The cover of Collin Hansen's 2008 book *Young, Restless, Reformed: A Journalist's Journey with the New Calvinists* depicts a cartoon-style character wearing a black t-shirt that is emblazoned with the words, "Jonathan Edwards is My Homeboy."[1] *Christianity Today* magazine, too, had a similar theme in the September 2009 edition in which the cover depicts an illustration of John Calvin wearing the same anachronistic slogan on a button pinned to his overcoat: "Jonathan Edwards is My Homeboy."

In the aforementioned book, Hansen chronicles the resurgence of interest in Reformed theology in general and such contemporary Calvinistic preachers as John Piper, John MacArthur, and Albert Mohler in particular. Here, Hansen also recounts the parallel renewal of interest in many dead theologians of a Reformed persuasion as well, including the subject of this essay, Jonathan Edwards (1703–1758). In his chapter entitled "Big Man on Campus," Hansen tells readers of the unlikely resurgence of concentration not only in terms of the academic study of the Northampton sage, but also the shocking renewal of attention to Edwards's writings among laypersons, church groups, and collegiate evangelicals such as among the burgeoning number of those who participate in Reformed University Fellowship (RUF) groups across the nation. Much of this interest in Edwards is undoubtedly, as Hansen correctly observers, directly due to the notable homage paid to Edwards himself by his popularizers, particularly John Piper. Apparently the "homeboy" t-shirt is a real thing too. A simple Google search for this item returns a number of online retailers that actually sell this and many other similar shirts and products featuring the wigged Puritan.[2]

In my early thirties at the time Hansen's book was written, I was in the exact demographic group that the journalist was talking about when he wrote. Part of the reason the church I pastor today in Brooksville Florida does well at attracting young twenty and thirty-somethings to our congregation is that we are still riding the wave of Reformed

[1] Cover illustration, Hansen 2008

Fig. 4: JE is my Homeboy

[2] For instance, Zazzle.com features nearly this exact item depicted on the cover of Hansen's book as does Café Press. Another company, Missionalwear.com features an entire line of Edwards-related items, including beer mugs featuring the famed Awakening preacher.

renewal that Hansen identified eight years ago. For instance, we recently did a summer study entitled "Dead Theologians Society" (it included Jonathan Edwards of course) that was so successful—even among younger parents with busy households—that we had to scramble room assignments just to find a location big enough for this "small group."

I will readily admit that part of the reason why I devoted the last three years of my life to studying Jonathan Edwards for my doctoral dissertation at Reformed Theological Seminary was because I became intrigued with Edwards through the impassioned preaching of John Piper. I began my quest to study and learn from Edwards (ironically in 2008, the very year Hansen wrote) and have not let go of this captivating figure from American religious history since. But in my time studying Edwards, especially in the past three years as my doctoral research crested, I inadvertently stumbled upon some idiosyncrasies in Edwards's thoughts and writings that began to bother me just a bit.[3] Was he really our "homeboy" as the t-shirts suggest? Among those idiosyncrasies of concern were his doctrine of justification, which was often asserted to be too "Roman Catholic,"[4] his rather eccentrically expressed doctrine of "continuous creation,"[5] and his flirtation with panentheism.[6]

Part of the reason I had not noticed these things in his writings before is that they do not always readily appear in his published works and sermons intentionally crafted for the public eye. Most of my readings had focused tightly there. More than that, the extant collection of Edwards's writings is so voluminous that even in a doctoral dissertation, it is difficult to take in all that he has written. Some of these unusual concepts that are considered theologically marginal were hidden in his *Miscellanies*, that is, Edwards's hundreds of tightly categorized and well organized personal notes that the Northampton pastor studiously maintained in private notebooks.[7] The *Miscellanies* are, after all, Edwards's private musings. Some include rough sketches and outlines for book ideas that Edwards ultimately hoped to bring before the public eye. But most of these entries he assumed would never see the light of day.

True enough, there are portions of Edwards's writings, both public and private, where he sounds, well, strange. In places, he didn't talk like many readers (then and now) think a Reformed theologian should talk. In some ways, especially in his *Miscellanies*, it seems that Edwards was either wandering alone in the meadow in terms of the way he expressed certain ideas, often ignoring the established vocabulary by which traditional conceptions had been expressed, or else he was straying into some forbidden territories that other Reformed theologians have been reticent to go. Certainly, Edwards's orthodoxy

[3] I should thank my dissertation adviser, Dr. Michael Allen, for pointing some of them out to me.

[4] See Josh Moody's essay "Edwards and Justification Today" (Moody, 2012, pp. 20–21)

[5] Oliver Crisp has a masterful examination of this doctrine in his chapter on "Ontology" among other places in his work *Jonathan Edwards on God and Creation* (Crisp, 2012)

[6] This too is covered well by Crisp in the penultimate chapter entitled "Panentheism" (Crisp, 2012, p. 138–63). Other doctrines of Jonathan Edwards have been challenged as well. Perry Miller, largely credited for the renewal of Edwards research in academic quarters asserted that Edwards rejected Covenant Theology. See Christopher Atwood, *Jonathan Edwards's Doctrine of Justification: A New Reading of Edwards's Treatises, Sermons, and Miscellanies* (Atwood, 2014, p. 20). Later research by subsequent scholars has largely shown this to be false. Other doctrines of Jonathan Edwards that have been challenged from time to time include his doctrine of the Trinity and, as his own dismissal from the Northampton Church shows, his understanding of the Lord's Supper.

[7] For more on the *Miscellanies*, their contents and compilation, see George Marsden, *Jonathan Edwards: A Life* (Marsden, 2003, p. 59).

will have to be held up to the light of examination for all who think him a reliable guide and plumb line for Reformed theology.[8]

One of the problems, of course, is being able to decipher what Jonathan Edwards—the man within the man—actually believed. Should greater weight be placed upon those writings which Edwards intentionally prepared for publication, or those private musings that he kept for himself? This is a genuine debate among Jonathan Edwards scholars. Those who argue the latter do so for the reason that they believe Edwards likely felt less restraint in his private thought life than in the public eye, and that the pressures of conformity that he felt in the pulpit and in published materials were lessened when alone in the study. In other words, he felt freer to be truly himself. However, like many others, I actually think the opposite is true.[9] I would argue that the "real" Edwards is the one who put what he truly intended to say in those well-prepared packages that he sent to the printer's shop. It is my working assumption in this essay that when Edwards sounds strange (possibly even heretical) in his private writings, it is often because he has not fully worked out his thinking in pen quite yet, a habit that he demonstrates over a lifetime of work. In this way, Edwards's *Miscellanies* can be thought of as freehand sketches before the master painter really takes up easel and palette to paint his masterpiece. In point of fact, Edwards almost always thought with his pen in his hand, and the extant manuscripts that we have today exhibit the bald truth that Edwards would sometimes work and rework a thought in various places until he crafted exactly what he wanted to say. Once he formulated an idea more concretely, however, he stuck with it, defending it staunchly for the rest of his life. In this way, it is his published words that take dominion in establishing his true thought.

In this essay I will ask one very important question that all young, restless, and Reformed evangelicals (to borrow Hansen's phrase) should consider: *Are you sure Jonathan Edwards is your homeboy?* What about Edwards's doctrine of justification; does it really verge on an amalgamation between Protestant and Roman Catholic theology? Does Edwards actually place too much emphasis on works and inherent righteousness to the neglect of the classical Reformed doctrine of *sola fide*? What in the world is Edwards's doctrine of "continuous creation" anyway? And what of the recurring assertion by many, including Oliver Crisp, that Edwards is a panentheist?[10] Is this true? If so, should his writings be rejected wholesale by today's Reformed evangelicals, or does his conception of God's relationship to the universe stay safely within the pale of historic orthodoxy?

I will attempt to do three things. First, I will show several of the ways that Jonathan Edwards is, in fact, a reliable guide and sage within the broader Reformed tradition. Here, I will argue that Edwards is

[8] To be fair, there are plenty of others who see very little to be concerned about in Edwards. Kyle Strobel gives a learned defense of Edwards's orthodoxy claiming that his reading of Edwards "allows Edwards to be what he claims to be, an orthodox Reformed theologian" rather than a philosopher-theologian (in that order) as Sang Hyun Lee, Perry Miller and others have made him out to be. See *Jonathan Edwards's Theology: A Reinterpretation* (Strobel, 2014, p. 91). Further, Strobel says Edwards was "a creative thinker working within a broadly Reformed/Puritan framework, and most of his provocative conclusions are creative reworkings of the theology handed down to him" (Strobel, 2014, p. 210). Charles Hodge, after articulating the doctrinal convictions of Jonathan Edwards in his *Systematic Theology* concludes that Edwards was consistent with the Westminster Confession of Faith and the Heidelberg Catechisms, even though he "initiated certain departures from some points of the Reformed faith" (Atwood, 2014, p. 13).

[9] For instance, Christopher Atwood says, "Although the relative significance assigned to Edwards's published works remains controversial, it seems reasonable that Edwards's published works ought to take precedence over semi-private rumination" (Atwood, 2014, p. 76). Josh Moody agrees with this sentiment. He says, "Only Edwards's published works, by his own intention, during his own lifetime, reveal with certainty what he wanted to say. Perhaps Edwards has hidden opinions in his notebooks not consistent with his preaching and writing, but the majority of Edwards scholarship has long shown that not to be the case" (Moody, 2012, p. 31).

[10] See especially Oliver Crisp, *Jonathan Edwards on God and Creation*, (Crisp, 2012, pp. 138–63)

exactly what he thought himself to be: a defender of Calvinistic ortho-doxy in his own day; a day in which the doctrines of grace espoused by the Puritans and Reformers before him were losing ground to the challenges presented by deists, "Arminians," atheists, and other intel-lectual heirs of the Enlightenment. In the second section, I will attempt to discuss some of the areas in which Jonathan Edwards is—at the very least—eccentric compared to the received Calvinistic orthodoxy that Edwards inherited, and as espoused by the historically and con-fessionally informed writers. In this section, I will attempt to discuss Edwards's idiosyncrasies with particular reference to his doctrines of justification and continuous creation. In the third section, then, I will explore the charge that Edwards is a panentheist. If true, this will probably damage Edwards's reputation as the "homeboy" of many Reformed evangelicals to some degree. And if he is a panentheist, it will probably be a strong reason why we should be cautious about putting Edwards on too high of a pedestal in our minds as Reformed churchmen and churchwomen. Finally, in the conclusion, I will at-tempt to make some general comments to frame the whole subject of Edwards's orthodoxy, with pertinence to Jonathan Edwards's legacy as a Reformed folk hero. Here, we will consider whether or not his eccentric doctrines should be thought of as tarnishing his reputation to some degree, or whether Edwards should still hold a venerable place as a role model for young pastors, theologians, and laypersons in the broader Reformed community.

Part One: Jonathan Edwards as Defender of Calvinistic Ortho-doxy

In this first section, I would hope to show that Jonathan Edwards was in fact a Reformed theologian, safely working and ministering within the boundaries of orthodox, confessional Calvinism in most regards. For this reason, those who are drawn to Edwards as a sort of Reformed folk hero can breathe an immediate sigh of relief. He is, in fact, our "homeboy."

Although Edwards was never afraid to butt up against controversy in his own day, the primary matrix or paradigm of his thinking poses no problem to those of us who are of an historically Reformed persuasion. On a macro level, Edwards viewed the Bible as the inspired Word of God, saw salvation through Jesus Christ as the only way to salvation,[11] believed that that salvation was granted by grace through faith in the life, death and resurrection of Jesus Christ, preached the necessity of the new birth of regeneration, received and administered the sacraments of the Lord's Supper and Baptism, worked from a covenantal framework in terms of God's relationship to humanity,[12] and taught the so-called

[11] This, despite Gerald McDermott's at-tempt to portray Edwards as open to the possibility of universalism in his article "A Possibility of Reconciliation: Jonathan Edwards and the Salvation of Non-Christians," in *Edwards in Our Time: Jonathan Edwards and the Shaping of Amer-ican Religion,* (Lee and Guelzo, 1999, pp. 173–202). In my own view, almost every attempt by the author to show that Ed-wards may have been theoretically open to universalism fails seriously in this arti-cle.

[12] See Edwards's "Observations Concern-ing the Scripture Oeconomy of the Trinity, and Covenant of Redemption" in *Treatise on Grace and Other Posthumous Writings In-cluding Observations on the Trinity* (Helm, 1971)

"Five Points."[13]

By and large, his beliefs were confessional. Although Edwards was a Congregationalist and was not required to subscribe to the Westminster Confession in the same formal way that Presbyterians do, he told his friend John Erskine in Scotland in a written correspondence that theoretically this would be no problem, for he "had no difficulty accepting 'the substance of the Westminster Confession.' "[14] Edwards was also known to teach the Shorter Catechism to his own children, believing it to be a sound teaching tool for Christian education.[15] Although references to confessional documents like the Westminster Confession and Heidelberg Catechism are quite rare in his writings and sermons, the evidence shows that he did not see himself at great variance with the confessional orthodoxy of his Reformed forefathers and Presbyterian contemporaries, if he saw himself at variance with them at all.

How Edwards viewed his own theological preferences is also greatly important. As to his predilections for theological literature, he said in a letter to his friend Joseph Bellamy that the renowned Reformed divines Peter Van Mastricht and Francis Turretine are "both excellent."[16] Turretine, he says, excels in the area of polemics and the Five Points of Calvinism, but Mastricht's theology he believed to be unparalleled in "divinity in general, doctrine, and practice" and even goes so far as to say that "it is much better than Turretine, or any other book in the world, excepting the Bible in my opinion."[17] Both of these authors are safely within the bounds of Reformed orthodoxy, and the mere fact that Edwards treasured their writings tells us a good bit about his preferences, orientation, and convictions as a theologian.

There is no doubt that Jonathan Edwards saw himself as a defender of historic Calvinism, and as such, perceived himself to be an orthodox Reformed theologian. He said as much in so many words in several places. This, too, is of no little importance in establishing Edwards's Reformed *bona fides*. In his introduction to *The Freedom of the Will*, for instance, Edwards directly acknowledges that, although he was not personally dependent on John Calvin as any authority to whom he must conform—and sometimes even disagreed with Calvin's interpretation in places—he nevertheless believed Calvin's views generally to be most biblical and perceived them to be under heavy attack in his own day.[18] It was due to this increasing attack, as he perceived it, that he wrote this masterpiece and others of his works. We will speak more of that below.

Edwards lived in a day in which the Protestant orthodoxy that he inherited not only from divines such as Van Mastricht and but also from his own direct family members—his own father Timothy Edwards and his famous paternal grandfather Solomon Stoddard were

[13] See for instance the conclusion to *Freedom of the Will* (*WJE* 1:430f)

[14] Marsden 2003, pp. 362–63

[15] Marsden 2003, p. 321

[16] Smith et al. 2005, pp. 304–05

[17] Smith et al. 2005, pp. 304–05

[18] He says, for example, "The term Calvinistic is, in these days among most, a term or greater reproach than the term Arminian, yet I should not take it at all amiss to be called a Calvinist, for distinction's sake; though I utterly disclaim a dependence on Calvin, or believing the doctrines which I hold, because he believed and taught them, and cannot justly be charged with believing in everything just as he taught" (*WJE* 1:131).

both Calvinistic Puritans of forceful persuasion—was being directly challenged. Those challenges to Calvinistic orthodoxy, as Edwards perceived them, were Arianism, Deism, Socinianism, Atheism, and "Arminianism," the latter being Edwards's catch-all term for anyone who dissented from more strident articulations of the doctrines of grace. He routinely described Arminianism and its implications as "pernicious."[19] He has nary a positive word to say about any of these categories in any of his writings or correspondences. If we can partially establish what a man is for by what he is against, then we can be certain that Edwards repudiated the humanity-exalting ideas burgeoning in his day as rippling results of the Enlightenment.

Jonathan Edwards's most important early sermon is entitled "God Glorified in Man's Dependence," which he preached in Boston on July 8, 1731. This sermon is significant because Edwards was taking a very public "shot across the bow" from an early age at those whom he perceived to be slipping from Calvinistic moorings. This sermon was heard by many of the influential Boston clergymen, and its point was clear: any other scheme which denigrates the absolute sovereignty of God by emphasizing the freedom and liberty of man is to be rejected, and should be shouted down from the pulpits of faithful men. Themes of sovereign grace would abound in his preaching ministry throughout his life, echoing the themes and emphases of *God Glorified*.

Moreover, when we consider the literary intention of every major work of Jonathan Edwards published within his own lifetime, it becomes apparent that almost without exception, Edwards was attempting to defend traditional Christianity from its Enlightenment critics at every turn. Edwards attempted to enlarge his defense of Christian orthodoxy at broader and broader levels throughout his career of literary production. One way to look at the canon of his published writings is to see them in an ever-expanding, cone-like trajectory, inasmuch as he defends Christianity at more and more basic levels. His earlier works primarily concentrated on defending the revivals, both local and regional. His later works, however, especially those written during his missionary endeavors in Stockbridge, took on more and more globally important issues for those of the Reformed faith, defending staple Calvinistic pillars doggedly.

Consider. Of those early works that Edwards purposefully brought to the press, it is clear that the Northampton sage crafted his initial theological project around the defense of local and regional revivals: *A Faithful Narrative* (1737) was written to illustrate sovereign grace as it related to the early localized Northampton revival in the middle of the 1730's. *Distinguishing Marks* (1741) was written to validate the broader works of renewing grace in the early parts of the then-expanding Great Awakening. *Some Thoughts Concerning the Present Revival of Religion in*

[19] *WJE* 1:131

New England (1742) was written to balance claims about the validity of the colonies-wide revivals both against its detractors and its overly-zealous enthusiasts.

By the time Edwards was relegated to the margins, so to speak, in the wilderness as a mature missionary to the Indians in Stockbridge, his defense of the Christian faith (read: historic Calvinism) became more and more directed towards primary, foundational loci of Reformed conviction. This would seem to show that Edwards perceived more and more as he aged that the very future of the Reformed movement in the Americas depended upon a rigorous defense of orthodoxy in his generation. The *Freedom of the Will* (1754) argued for a compatibilist understanding of necessity and human will, maintaining (contra Arminian views) that both man and God are bound to act according to necessity. He differentiated between natural and moral necessity,[20] and robustly defended Calvinism against "Arminianism," even if he parted ways from the manner in which Martin Luther had worked through issues of divine sovereignty and human responsibility generations before in *The Bondage of the Will*. The conclusion to *Freedom of the Will* is particularly Calvinistic, arguing through each one of the points of the T.U.L.I.P. acronym in turn. What could be more Calvinistic than that?

[20] *WJE* 1:156

His *The End for Which God Created the World* (1755) attempted to give a reason for why God created in the first place, since God Himself is sovereign over all things and stands in no need of human applause or approval. Here, it becomes clear that Edwards hoped to defend the notion that God is the first cause and last end of all things. God is the center of all existence, not humanity, he averred. Again, massive themes consistent with Calvinism are present throughout. In *The Nature of True Virtue*, Edwards acknowledges that Reformed piety retains a vigorous understanding of ethical imperatives, arguing that Christian morality is fundamentally contingent upon a "benevolence to Being in general."[21] This would be necessary for Edwards, as he knew in his day (and our own) that one of the great objections to Calvinism is that it fosters antinomianism, or lawless living. This objection, Edwards forcefully repudiated by showing just how intrinsic Christian ethics are to a biblical worldview.

[21] *WJE* 8:540

In the last piece of literature that Edwards prepared for the press in his own lifetime, *Original Sin* (1758), the preacher-turned-missionary had determined that he must now write the treatise that he probably hoped he would never have to write. He needed to defend even a most basic understanding of the nature of humanity as sinful, fallen creatures. In a largely polemic work, Edwards quoted copiously from John Taylor's book *The Scripture Doctrine of Original Sin Proposed to Free and Candid Examination*. Here, Edwards labored strenuously to disabuse his readers of Taylor's increasingly popular humanism. Often quoting Taylor paragraph by paragraph, Edwards worked to defend the Calvinistic doctrine of original sin (or total depravity as it is variously termed) from his opponent's logical and biblical errors before it was too late and further precious theological ground was lost to the advance of Enlightenment ideology.

In all of these ways, then, it is obvious that Jonathan Edwards's Calvinistic *bona fides* are solidly defensible and patently manifest. His agreement with the substance of the Confessions, his admiration for renowned Protestant divines like Van Mastricht, Turretine, John Owen and others, his rigorous defense of the faith "once and for all handed down" to him by his father and grandfather in the face of a generation of sweeping change, and, indeed, even his massive literary theological project can all be summoned to testify to his defense as an orthodox, "truly Reformed" theologian. Without any doubt, we can be sure that in the above ways, Jonathan Edwards can be considered a folk hero for young churchmen and women. So it is settled then: "Jonathan Edwards is our homeboy." Right?

And yet it is ironic that Jonathan Edwards is brought under the great light of suspicion for two of his views which are intrinsically tied to his role in the revivals and his attempts to defend Calvinism. The first area of suspicion that we should mention is his view on justification, a most central doctrine indeed for the historic Reformed community. The irony is that it is in this very sermon series that he preached that helped to launch the local revival in Northampton in the mid-1730's which calls his views of justification into question. The other irony is that it is the very document in which Edwards most clearly attempted to defend one of the pillars of Calvinism, his 1758 work *Original Sin,* which brought his doctrine of "continuous creation" also into contentious criticism. We will consider now each of these doctrines in part two.

Part Two: Part Two: Jonathan Edwards as Innovator and Eccentric

So far, I have worked to show that, generally considered, Jonathan Edwards is safely in the camp of a Reformed Calvinist. No big deal. So what is all the fuss about these challenges to his orthodoxy and his theological innovations? In this section, we will briefly look at two of his doctrines that have been challenged for their alleged unfaithfulness to the Reformed tradition: justification and creation. Later, in the third section, we will look at the charge of his being a panentheist, which, if true, may be the most serious problem of all for Edwards devotees.

Justification

Jonathan Edwards wrote and preached considerably on justification as all Protestant ministers inevitably do. This was in fact the subject of his Master's thesis in 1722 as well as the subject of not a few of his *Miscellanies*.[22] He also preached a significant sermon series on justification in 1734 which was, according to some, (including Edwards himself), the spark that lit the fire of the local Northampton revival. A few years later, this sermon series would be prepared for the printer's shop, and the rather long sermonic orations would take on the form of a 1738 treatise in six parts.

Briefly stated, the controversy regarding Edwards's formulation of justification has to do with the way that he emphasised certain aspects of the doctrine without using the established frameworks set before him by his forbearers in the faith. Not only that, but certain "litmus test" expressions and thought patterns are notably absent from his writings on this topic, bringing them under heavy scrutiny. In all fairness, it is probably true that contemporary debates about justification and the so-called New Paul Perspective have also caused modern academics to work feverishly to "claim" Edwards to their own side, further exacerbating the controversy.[23] In fact, it is interesting to note that Reformed evangelicals of previous generations, before the NPP debate came about (such as John Gerstner, Martin Lloyd-Jones, and Charles Hodge)[24] found little or no fault with Edwards's conception of justification.

Christopher Atwood, whose 2014 dissertation tackles this difficult subject very capably, identifies several such nuances that make Edwards "weird." First, Edwards does not often speak with the typical clear distinction between justification and sanctification as most Reformed thinkers do. In fact, he doesn't frequently speak of sanctification at all, except when he is quoting Scripture or other writers in his journals.[25] More than that, Edwards is far more likely to talk about "inherent righteousness" than most Reformed thinkers are comfortable doing. The term "inherent" in general seems to have at least some superficial similarity to the Roman Catholic doctrine of "infused righteousness," repudiated by the Westminster Confession 11.1—at least according to some critics. Also, Edwards does not seem to think of faith as the "instrument" of justification (WCF 11.2),[26] but rather tends to speak more in terms of the doctrine of Union with Christ,[27] making justifying faith less punctilliar in time, and broadening and extending it over the lifetime of the believer, culminating in a final justification that encapsulates one's whole life. Complicating matters, Edwards does not seem to think of faith as a gift given to the believer, but rather as that which apprehends Christ in relational union. While standard Reformed

[22] The *Miscellanies* can be found in a searchable format at http://edwards.yale.edu/research/misc-index.

[23] This is a point brought up by Douglas Sweeney in his article "Justification by Faith Alone? A Fuller Picture of Edwards's Doctrine" (Moody, 2012, pp. 129–30).
[24] Atwood 2014, pp.12–13

[25] Atwood 2014, p.243

[26] Atwood 2014, p.228
[27] *WJE* 19:143

[28] Consider such texts as Eph 2:8–9; Acts 11:8; John 3:27; Phil 1:29; and Acts 18:27.

[29] Moody 2012, 33–34

[30] Edwards has a very serious discussion about the necessity of works in *Justification by Faith Alone* (WJE 19:236).

[31] Atwood 2014, p. 172

[32] WJE 19:154

[33] Atwood 2014, pp. 1–5

[34] WJE 19:139

views tend to see even faith itself as a gift,[28] Edwards does boldly distance himself from the tradition by viewing faith as more of an act (not a meritorious one, but an act nonetheless) subsuming into it other expressions such as: repentance, love to Christ, sorrow for sin, trusting God's promises, and evangelical obedience.[29] Finally, in a Jamesean fashion, Edwards is sure to emphasise the necessity of works[30]—not as the cause of justification, but as that which is most "fit" and "beautiful." In this way, as Atwood states succinctly, Edwards guarded justification "lest conversion be over-championed and a holy life be cheapened."[31]

These latter terms, "fitness" and "beauty" are, for Edwards, quintessential to his theology as a whole. Edwards believed that salvation is a process in which the entirety of a person's transformation has a certain symmetry, balance, and rightness to it.[32] Just as a human face is considered most beautiful in a woman, for instance, when her eyes, cheekbones, forehead, nose and lips are in a right and natural proportion (and one is ugly when they are not!) Edwards saw good works as the proper balance and proportion to saving faith. For this reason, they are absolutely essential—not as earning salvation—but garnishing it properly and fitly. Probably he emphasized this balance more than other Reformed theologians, since this concept is intrinsic to his theology as a whole.

All of this leads Christopher Atwood to posit in his excellent dissertation that Edwards held to an orthodox, but lesser known, view of justification known as *duplex iusticia*,[33] or having a double formal cause—the first a justification by faith, but later a subsequent justification by works, which corresponding acts of obedience balance, spring forth from naturally, and radiate spontaneously from the new nature imparted to the elect person by the living principle of the Holy Spirit now dwelling within her. In fact, Edwards does use some language that would substantiate this claim. Late in the work, he states:

> To be justified is to be approved of and accepted. But a man may be said to be approved and accepted in two respects: the one is to be approved really, and the other is to be approved and accepted declaratively. Justification is twofold.[34]

If all of this sounds strange, the reader would do well to simply read his 1734/38 work *Justification by Faith Alone*, especially chapters one and two. Like many Edwards works, this one begins with very clear definitions and concepts that will support the whole argument. There the reader will find, along with typically Edwardsean language of "fitness," "beauty," "congruity" and the like (somewhat strange language to many modern Reformed evangelicals to be sure), a rather readable and clear defense of the Protestant doctrine of justification. Readers without a "New Paul Perspective axe to grind" will find there a rather lucid and straightforward insistence that justification is in fact by faith alone (despite allegations that it is due to a Romanesque infused righteousness), that it is received and not earned by works of the law,[35] that it is of a forensic nature, and other important Reformational distinctives. Edwards is very clear that justification is a gift given to the elect due to no goodness or moral rectitude in their being,[36] and that it is something imputed, reckoned, or counted to the believer.[37] Instead of being earned or deserved, justification is won for the believer by the active and passive obedience of Jesus Christ, and on that merit alone. These constructs are all well acknowledged and embraced by the Reformed tradition.

So, does Edwards represent an orthodox view of justification as understood by the Calvinistic orthodoxy? I think so. So apparently do Atwood and Moody, given that we acknowledge Edwards added some unusual twists to the conversation.[38] Probably the reason why this doctrine is so contentious is not that Edwards is unorthodox *per se*, but rather that he seems to talk over and past the tradition. He eschews tried and worn verbal patterns (i.e. faith is the instrumental cause of justification), instead opting for more organic formulations that often owed more allegiance to his own overall theological system than confessional terminology, even if he doesn't explain that burden overtly to the reader. Sometimes it even feels that Edwards is making his points to keep his own system coherent rather than to make sense to the listener or reader, assuming that they too knew what he wrote and said in many other places. To make an analogy, if the doctrine of justification were a railroad, Edwards presents a parallel track to the tradition, going where it goes—always staying an arm's span away— but without utilizing the same language, and thus becoming a mere repeater of the tradition. Instead, Edwards presents other emphases that are foundational to his own theology (works being "fit," "congruent" and "beautiful," symmetrical to faith, etc.) which are not often utilized by others of the same tradition. Doubtless, he is bold in rejecting the confessional language of instrumentality, but he does so merely to emphasize union with Christ, and motivated out of a desire to be clearer than, rather than contradictory to, the tradition. Whether or not he is successful in that intention, I will let other readers decide.

Continuous Creation

A second area of concern for those who study Edwards is his unusual conception of the creation of the world. But whereas his understanding of justification had more in common with the Reformed tradition than divergence from it (without slavishly using the same words and emphasizing the same concepts like a broken record), here we will probably find that Jonathan Edwards presents something else entirely.

[35] In fact, he takes quite a bit of space to show how "works of the law" does not only mean the ceremonial law, but all strands of the law, including the moral law. This point he belabors to make clear that justification is quite apart from anything that a man can say or do to please God and therefore justify himself. See Jonathan Edwards, *Justification by Faith Alone* (WJE 19:167–82).

[36] WJE 19:147–49

[37] WJE 19:149

[38] Moody 2012, pp. 42–43

If I am reading the Westminster Confession chapter four correctly, and if the Westminster Confession does properly represents the mainstream Reformed tradition, then we should look for an understanding of creation in Edwards as being completed "in the space of six day, and all very good." Moreover, we should find that the creation actually *exists* as a material universe, made out of tangible "stuff" that really subsists apart from and distinct from God, (although entirely dependent on Him in every way), maintaining a clear delineation between Creator and the creation. In fact, in my own estimation, that Creator/creation distinction seems axiomatic of Reformed understandings of ontology: God created the world by the word of His power, but that world cannot be confused with the creator as He stands over it, holding providential dominion over all things. The fact that creation is *ex nihilo* is assumed as a matter of course in Reformed orthodoxy. All matter that exists, as I believe the tradition rightly teaches, exists in a way that is directly dependent upon God, and yet nothing existed prior to God's having created it.

But this is not exactly what we find in Edwards. In fact, his conception of creation is a strange animal indeed. If, according to my prior analogy, Edwards's doctrine of justification was like a parallel railroad track running alongside the tradition, here in his doctrine of creation, Edwards could probably be pictured walking out in the meadow some distance from the tracks in a rather lonely way.

Some background is necessary here. When Edwards wrote his polemical work *Original Sin* (his last published work before his death) as a response to John Taylor's rejection of the doctrine of total depravity, he did so with one primary goal in mind: to uphold the Reformed conception of hamartiology—mankind is dead in sin, and a slave to it. The way he defended this doctrine, though, becomes more and more unusual, even though the treatise begins in a rather straightforwardly Reformed way. In *Original Sin*, Edwards refutes Taylor's work in detail, often quoting significant portions of it at length. Nearly the entire work is polemical, and rigorously exegetical, working through a number of important biblical passages, especially those in the books of Genesis and Romans. Edwards defends the Reformed doctrine of depravity robustly, even reasserting the depravity and damnability of unregenerate infants. But while Edwards's defense of Calvinism here is orthodox, his methodology is innovative to be sure in the latter portions. Rather than emphasizing either an inherited guilt (i.e. Augustinian) position, or the federal headship position (i.e. Calvin and the Westminster Divines), Edwards instead utilizes an argument from his unique conception of "continuous creation," ironically putting him at odds with many in the broader Reformed community.

Let's allow Oliver Crisp to define "continuous creation":

This is the view according to which God creates the world out of nothing, whereupon it momentarily ceases to exist, to be replaced by a facsimile that has incremental differences built into it to account for what appear to be motion and change across time. This, in turn, is annihilated, or ceases to exist, and is replaced by another facsimile world that has incremental differences built into it to account to be what appear to be motion and change across time, and so on.[39]

[39] Crisp 2012, p. 25

In a nutshell, Edwards taught that God is continually creating and recreating the universe every instant. Every moment that God creates, He does so again just an instant later. The very instant God creates, He also recreates the entire world again, with each successive manifestation just slightly progressed from the last. In this way, Edwards thought he was upholding the doctrine of providence. Without God upholding the universe constantly in this way, all being would cease to "be." But the payload in terms of his argument for the doctrine of original sin was on the back end: By arguing that God is constantly creating (or recreating) reality every instant, supporting the universe by His decrees of providence, Edwards argues that there is a linear, unbroken continuity between Adam and all his descendants by which God views all of humanity as one. By analogy, just as the human cells of an older man have been entirely reconstituted from who he once was 40 years earlier, or as a mature oak tree is entirely reconstituted from the acorn in which it once existed in seminal form—and yet they are regarded as existentially one and the same entity—so also has the entire human race been reconstituted in physical form since Adam. Nevertheless, just as God sovereignly ordains to reckon the tree as the same being or thing as the acorn, and the aged man as the same person he once was, so also (Edwards argues) God regards the culpability of Adam as being possessed by all mortals. Thus, God decrees to view them as one continual race from Adam, and his guilt as the guilt of all. In this way, Edwards could argue that Adam's sin was beholden to all of us— humanity being an unbroken line of continuously recreated sinners, each directly tied to our forefather Adam. While Edwards's motives to defend Calvinistic orthodoxy were well appreciated by traditional Reformed theologians, his innovative rationale for argumentation has been much more controversial.

Oliver Crisp gives a fantastic analogy of how this worked in Edwards's mind:

Edwards's doctrine of God's relation to the world he creates is rather like that of a projectionist and the motion picture he is responsible for projecting onto the theatrical screen; each world stage is similar to a discrete photograph still that is one of many stills in a series, segued together in a sequence on a reel that is then projected onto the silver screen of a movie theater, giving the illusion of continuous action across time....Creation comprises a set of world-stages that God orders into a series as he sees fit. And God is the only causal agent acting in this way. Creatures are merely occasions of this divine act.[40]

In this way, however, Edwards seems to be working further and further away from creation as traditionally understood as an existing substance-and-material entity. Edwards drives this concept further and further away from a literally existing creation—made of real "stuff" (for lack of a more precise theological term!) and closer and closer to a neo-platonic notion similar to idealism. Idealism, to define the term more fully, teaches that all that is exists merely as "ideas," bundles of properties, which according to Edwards, exist exclusively in the mind of an all-powerful God.[41] In other words, creation *ex nihilo* was not a once-and-for-all event wherein God brings into being all matter that is, but rather an infinitely repeating process that transpires perhaps even thousands of times (maybe even an infinite number of times) each and every second. While traditional views of creation allow for particles, molecules and other "stuff" to be reassigned and relocated by God—as, for example, in that the human body contains entirely different cells at age 40 than it did at age six—yet it is usually held that all the matter that comprises the universe came to be at the original creation. New stars are being formed, but the gasses, particulates and energy already came to be at creation and are merely being reassigned and reorganized by God. But Edwards seems to be saying something very different: he seems to be arguing a philosophy of occasionalism wherein what is, is actually existent in the mind of God only, and not in any distinct way a part of another "reality" distinct from God. In this way, the traditional Reformed understanding of the Creator/creation distinction is blurred if not erased entirely.

Oliver Crisp rightly concludes, then, that "Such an interpretation also better comports with the picture of Edwards as an intellectual magpie, who sought to synthesize aspects of the early Enlightenment thinking with post-Reformation scholastic metaphysics."[42] At this point we can begin to see why I am suggesting in this paper that Edwards is a Reformed eccentric. To quote Crisp once more, "Edwards's ontology is a rather strange thing, there is no denying that."[43]

So now we are in a bit of a quandary. While Edwards has proved himself to be a venerable Calvinist in many other ways—a champion of Calvinism even—there seems to be more of an Enlightenment emphasis and infiltration into the man's thinking than appears superficially on the surface. But before we decide to brush this one eccentric doctrine off as an anomaly, we have to see how far this thought progresses in Edwards's thinking. Like *Alice in Wonderland,* we must see how deep the rabbit hole goes. Does he take this too far? If Edwards views all of creation as merely existing in the mind of God—and that God is the only true substance in existence—is creation then a part of, or extension of, God in some way? To frame the question more bluntly: *Is Edwards also a panentheist?*

Part Three: Part Three: Panentheism

"Panentheism" is, according to the *New Dictionary of Theology,* "the view that the universe is God, though God is more than the universe. It should be clearly distinguished from pantheism, in which God and the universe are strictly identical."[44] According to pantheism, rocks are divine, rivers are divine, and the stars are divine, too. This is certainly the stronger of categories. But in the former view (panentheism) it is more proper to say that the universe is an extension of God's power or works, although God Himself exists on a higher plain and apart from creation. This is important, because "For the panentheist, God has an identity of his own, that is, he is something the universe is not."[45] For the panentheist, if the creation did not exist, God still would. But for the pantheist, if the creation dissipated or was destroyed, God himself, being subsumed within it, would no longer have any independent existence either.

Another definition of panentheism accepted by Oliver Crisp—who asserts that Edwards does in fact espouse this weaker of the two categories—is "the view according to which 'the being of God includes and penetrates the whole universe, so that every part exists in Him, but His being is more than, and not exhausted by, the universe.'"[46] True enough, I think we can see strains of panentheism in Edward's extant written works, although I doubt he ever used the term to describe himself.[47] In *The End for Which God Created the World,* for instance, Edwards is constantly talking about the universe as an "emanation" of God, often comparing it to the rays of the sun which have no existence apart from the sun itself. This is stock language in Edwards's writing and it is almost ubiquitous in this important treatise. In this way, Edwards will even speak of God "expanding Himself," or extending Himself so as to create that which remanates his own glory back to Him. This is the thesis of the book by which Edwards claims that God is ultimately glorified: God emanates His glory in creation by the act of creating, especially in the creation of intelligent creatures which apprehend his glory. And the creation remanates His glory back to Himself in joyful adoration. This language of emanation/remanation is found constantly throughout *The End,* and the purpose of creation then (as Edwards explains it) drives towards the ultimate glory of God through happily creating and immediately receiving the appropriate happiness of the intelligent creatures in return. Once again, we see the doctrine of "beauty" or "congruity" present here, and we notice the strong framework of "fitness" and "symmetry" in this entire concept.

[44] Ferguson et al. 1998, p. 486

[45] Ferguson et al. 1998, p. 486

[46] Crisp 2012, p. 140

[47] If he does, I am not aware of it. A search of the word "panentheism" in the *Works of Jonathan Edwards Online* at the Edwards Center at Yale University does not yield any results. I have not come across him using this term in my own readings of Edwards's extant works.

Borrowing from the language of the Apostle Paul, Edwards would have us to believe that it is in this way, i.e. emanation/remanation, that all things are "from Him and to Him and through Him" (Romans 11:36).

Drawing some preliminary conclusions from Edwards's doctrine of continuous creation, as well as from his idealism often expressed in his more philosophic *Miscellanies*[48] and his experimental pieces such as "The Mind" and "On Being" in which he attempted to wed his philosophy of metaphysics with his theological frameworks, we can see why Edwards has been charged with the label of being a panentheist. In "On Being," for instance, he directly says that the universe "exists nowhere but in the divine mind."[49] This is not typically Reformed language to be sure. Edwards would also say directly that, "The first Being, the eternal and infinite Being, is in effect, Being in general; *and comprehends universal existence*, as was observed before" (emphasis added).[50] Although this kind of expression strongly upholds the doctrine of God's providence, since the existence of the universe is directly dependent upon God's maintaining it instant by instant, it also tends to deny that the universe has any real or actual existence apart from God's conception of it. Since according to Edwards, the universe has no other existence besides as it exists as the idea of God, existing properly and most really in God's own mind and nowhere else, it is hard to make a clean differentiation between where God "stops" and where creation "begins." The world, for Edwards, as Crisp summarizes his thinking, "is a divine emanation ad extra like rays of the sun (which) are emanated by the sun or like waters of the fountain are emanated from the fountainhead."[51] He believed, according to Crisp's understanding of these texts, "that God and the world were distinct, but that the world is somehow contained 'in' God."[52] This latter portion is precisely the problem which takes Edwards away from the Reformed tradition of the doctrine of creation.

How exactly God and creation are distinct in Edwards's thinking is hard to discern. In "Miscellany" no. 697, Edwards says something that adds to the complexity of the puzzle,

> An infinite being, therefore, must be an all-comprehending being. He must comprehend in himself all being. That there should be another being underived and independent, and so no way comprehended, will argue him not to be infinite, because then there is something more. There is more entity. There is some entity beside what is in this being; and therefore, his entity cannot be infinite.[53]

I think we can see what Edwards is doing in the above quotation: he is trying to protect the absolute infinity of God who exists in and of himself. In God's pure aseity, He must exist in a way that is truly infinite and independent. But at the expense of God's infinity (which he upholds) he unintentionally minimizes the "goodness" of creation

[48] Such as "Miscellany" no. 697

[49] Crisp 2012, p. 144

[50] *The End for Which God Created the World*, quoted in (Crisp, 2012, p. 138)

[51] Crisp 2012, p. 163

[52] Crisp 2012, p. 140

[53] "Miscellany" no. 697 quoted in (Crisp, 2012, p. 140)

in forbidding it to simply be (or exist) in any real, substantial (read: material) way. Consequently, the universe seems to be part of God's own existence as His thoughts belong to His own quiddity.

We might be able to make an analogy here. (This is my own analogy, not one Edwards used, by the way.) Suppose that a man falls asleep and dreams. In his dream, he creates a vivid world quite different from the one in which he lives during the day. Since the dream world exists only as a figment of the man's imagination, it is safe to say that the world entirely exists in a manner in which it completely depends on the man. The dream is an extension of the man. But if his alarm clock rings and wakes him up, the world he created in his mind evaporates. He exists, even if the created world doesn't. There is no question that the man exists. The dream world, too, has real existence, if only in the man's mind. But the question as it pertains to panentheism is this: does the dream world actually exist in any real way *apart* from the man's mind, or is it merely an *extension* of the man himself? Is it possible to speak of the dream as having its own existence or is it merely a projection of the man's own being? To pose the question most directly as it pertains to Edwards's doctrine, where does the man's mind *end* and the reality of the dream *begin?* Or is there even a distinction at all?

If we can risk returning to the railroad metaphor one more time, I think at this point we see Jonathan Edwards getting off of the tracks of the Reformed tradition and making a perpendicular turn away from established, confessional Calvinism. He does seem to be butting up against the concept that the universe is actually part of God rather than having its own independent existence. How dangerous this detour is and how damaging it is to Edwards's reputation as a reliable sage and guide to today's Reformed evangelicals should be left to the reader to decide. In my own view, I find it disappointing that Edwards went so far afield from our received doctrinal inheritance on this issue, but some of these nuances are exactly what makes Edwards such an intriguing subject of study. He was rigorously traditional in some ways, but a bold innovator in others.

Conclusion: Edwards as a Reformed Eccentric

To conclude, we can find that his status as the New Calvinist's "home-boy" is established, but quite shaky in certain areas. He is definitely a Reformed eccentric, and should probably be classified as such. We can probably put his writings into three categories. First, there are many of Edwards's doctrines that are solid, reliable, and thoroughly Reformed. Probably the majority of his writings can safely go in this category. After reading Edwards for a little less than a decade, I find him to be orthodox, reliable, and trustworthy in general. Certainly his sermons are invaluable, and would make great fodder for young Reformed preachers like myself to ruminate over. Secondly, others of his doctrines are expressed with innovation, but should not be considered heterodox. His expressions of justification go into this category. I believe that Edwards is faithful to Scripture and to the Reformed tradition without becoming a parrot of the same. He expresses biblical truth in a way that is refreshing, honest, and consistent, even if phrased in different wording and boldly challenging the confessional tradition, not so much by contradicting it, but by attempting to bring clarity and balance in some areas that it perhaps lacks. But thirdly there are some areas of Edwards's works in which he departs from our received tradition, and I believe, from Biblical orthodoxy. His understanding of continuous creation is courageous and even invigorating to think about, but certainly lacks biblical support. His sources here are more drawn from Enlightenment thinking, neo-platonic conceptions of ontology, and his penchant for philosophical musings rather than Scripture. We can, of course, forgive this when it comes to his private journals and musings such as the *Miscellanies.* We owe him the liberty to be a free thinker, especially where he never imagined he would be held up to examination. Where can the man think "aloud" if not in his private papers that he never dreamed would be examined so critically by generations of Edwards scholars who he could not have even fathomed would be chasing down his every stoke of his pen? But we should be honest enough to also acknowledge that there are some stranger areas of his thinking that went too far. Edwards flirted with panentheism, and even succumbed to it in the views of many, failing to maintain in his metaphysical view of the universe a proper distinction between creation and God Himself, or even that the universe truly exists in any material or actual sense. Rather, in attempting to uphold the infinity of God, he inadvertently diminished the goodness of the creation that God sovereignly decreed to create with substantial matter.

Can Edwards truly be a folk hero for today's new generation of Calvinists? Yes, I think so. Especially in his bold preaching of the Word of God. So also in his love for, and even obsession with, revivals and revivalism. Here, he may be the clearest writer ever in print. But if we are to look for a philosopher who can articulate a thoroughly Reformed and confessional metaphysic, providing for us an ontology that fully comports with our confessional moorings, we would do well to look elsewhere.

In conclusion then, Jonathan Edwards is our Reformed, but eccentric, "homeboy."

Did Jonathan Edwards Help Inspire the Modern Missionary Movement?

OBBIE TYLER TODD

Edwards and Fuller

In June 1805, from Kettering, England, pastor Andrew Fuller wrote to American theologian Timothy Dwight concerning Fuller's honorary diploma from Yale College. Fuller had attained considerable renown across the Atlantic for his treatises, owing much to the theological heritage bequeathed to him by Dwight's grandfather, Jonathan Edwards. In this small letter, the reader discovers not only Edwards's influence upon Fuller, but upon Fuller's band of missionary compatriots as well: "The writings of your grandfather, President Edwards, and of your uncle, the late Dr. Edwards, have been food to me and many others. Our brethren Carey, Marshman, Ward, and Chamberlain, in the East Indies, all greatly approve of them."[1] The legacy of Jonathan Edwards flourished and found new expression in the theology and missiology of Andrew Fuller. In his defense of evangelistic Calvinism and Puritanical piety, the man Charles Spurgeon called the greatest theologian of his century summoned the works of Edwards in order to elucidate Scriptural principles for a modern church beginning to relinquish them.

For all of his doctrinal influence, the "theologian of the Great Commandment" also stirred Fuller to a deeper spirituality with his *Life of David Brainerd* (1749), a biography of an American missionary to the Delaware River Indians.[2] His impact is most evident in Fuller's *Memoirs of the Rev. Samuel Pearce* (1800). By comparing these two biographies in the realms of piety, evangelism, and particular redemption, this chapter will present Jonathan Edwards as a dominant influence upon the thought of Andrew Fuller. This thesis is consonant with Chris Chun's assertion that "Fuller's main contribution was to expand, implicate, and apply Edwardsean ideas in his own historical setting."[3] The following is an attempt to locate such ideas in both biographies

Fig. 5: Andrew Fuller (1754–1815)

[1] Haykin 2001, pp. 199–200

[2] Haroutunian 1944, pp. 361–77

[3] Chun 2008, p. 127

and to offer Edwards as a genuine inspiration for the Modern Missions Movement.

Two Eighteenth Century Calvinists

While both Edwards and Fuller lived in the same enlightened century, they also occupied both poles of it. Andrew Fuller was born in 1754—the year that Edwards's *Freedom of the Will* was published and four years before Edwards's death. Therefore the Congregationalist and the Particular Baptist were not contemporaries. However, their historical proximity benefited Fuller in his attempt to countervail the same eighteenth-century rationalism as his predecessor. Edwards's writings fueled Fuller's theological aims years after his death.[4] Before examining Fuller's memoirs and treatises, it is necessary to first hear from Fuller and those closest to him regarding Edwards and Brainerd. This will provide a much-needed texture with which to feel the words of all three men. For instance, Fuller took note of his critics who no doubt heard much of Edwards in his preaching:

> We have some who have been giving out, of late, that 'If Sutcliff and some others had preached more of Christ, and less of Jonathan Edwards, they would have been more useful.' If those who talked thus preached Christ half as much as Jonathan Edwards did, and were half as useful as he was, their usefulness would be double what it is.[5]

Fuller was unashamed in his admiration for the pastor from Northampton, Massachusetts. After all, Edwards's *Freedom of the Will* had helped him to reconcile evangelistic preaching with the divine sovereignty of Calvinism.[6] Edwards aided Fuller in his disavowal of the High Calvinism of John Gill and John Brine.[7] His *Religious Affections*, on the other hand, equipped Fuller to refute the Sandemanianism of men like Archibald McLean.[8] Fuller even boasted that Edwards's sermons on justification brought him "more satisfaction on that important doctrine than any human performance which I have read."[9]

[4] In 1775, Robert Hall of Arnsby recommended Edwards's *Freedom of the Will* to Fuller. Hall himself was greatly aided by this work, obvious in his own *Help to Zion's Travelers* (1781), a work that answered the 'Modern Question' with an affirmative. According to Hall, invitations to unregenerate sinners were completely compatible with the strictest Calvinism.

[5] Fuller 1988, 1:101

[6] In his second edition of *The Gospel Worthy of All Acceptation,* Fuller acknowledges his debt to Jonathan Edwards's *Inquiry into the Freedom of the Will* in distinguishing between natural and moral inability. Man's post-lapsarian natural abilities remain intact but are suppressed by his evil disposition to the things of God, resulting in a wicked aversion of the heart. Fuller concluded in his epochal work that God would not require of sinners that which was naturally impossible. However, man's inability to spiritual good was of the moral and criminal kind. The problem for sinners is not being able, but being willing. Therefore, all unregenerate sinners have a *duty* to repent of their sin and believe in the Gospel. Likewise, ministers have a *duty* to plead, invite, call, and command sinners to such repentance and faith. According to Fuller, the 'warrant of faith' espoused in High Calvinism was unscriptural and dependent upon 'enthusiasm' and not truth. One's faith is not founded upon the confidence in such faith, but a confidence in the work of Christ. In short, sinners are not to wait until they are elect, or 'warranted', to believe. Their election is confirmed by their repentance and faith in Christ.

[7] Fuller wrote that he "perceived...that the system of Bunyan was not the same with [Gill's]; for that while he [Bunyan] maintained the doctrines of election and predestination, he nevertheless held with the free offer of salvation to sinners without distinction." (Fuller, 1988, 1:15)

[8] On February 3, 1781, upon reading Edwards' *Religious Affections,* Fuller wrote, "I think I have never yet entered into the true idea of the work of the ministry...I think I am by the ministry, as I was by my life as a Christian before I read *Edwards on the Affections.*" (Fuller, 1988, 1:25). Fuller's *Strictures on Sandemanianism* explored the nature of faith against those who held that saving faith was by mere intellectual assent to biblical facts. According to Robert Sandeman, any virtue or holiness that pertained to faith necessarily destroyed the doctrine of sola fide. Fuller's work is considered a definitive response to the controversy, positing that belief is registered in the heart and not simply the mind. Edwardean language is pervasive throughout: "A spiritual perception of the glory of Divine things appears to be the first sensation of which the mind is conscious." A "bare faith" hardly passed for faith in Fuller's Edwardean mind. [9] Haykin 2001, pp. 199–200.

Still, Edwards's treatises and sermons were not the only sources of theological direction for Fuller. The name of David Brainerd was one he also held in high esteem. At Fuller's funeral, friend John Ryland, Jr. invoked Edwards's famous biography along with his *Affections*: "If I knew I should be with ... Fuller tomorrow, instead of regretting that I had endeavored to promote that religion delineated by Jonathan Edwards in his *Treatise on Religious Affections* and in his *Life of David Brainerd*, I would recommend his writings ... with the last effort I could make to guide a pen."[10] The reference to the New Jersey missionary at Fuller's funeral was apropos. After all, both men had given their lives in service to missions. Fuller had served as the founding secretary of the Baptist Missionary Society since 1792.[11] Since his disillusionment from the High Calvinism of his childhood pastor John Eve, Fuller had dedicated himself to the Great Commission.[12] Thankfully, the theology of Jonathan Edwards had helped to confirm and explicate what Fuller saw so clearly in Scripture.[13]

In his preface to *The Gospel Worthy of All Acceptation*, Fuller singularly answers the "Modern Question" in the positive.[14] Recalling his inspiration for the volume, he mentions Brainerd by name: "Reading the lives and labours of such men as Elliot, Brainerd, and several others, who preached Christ with so much success to the American Indians, had an effect upon him."[15] It was in his last year at Soham that Fuller wrote *A Gospel Worthy*. However, it was actually his removal to Kettering in 1782 that would spell the beginning of a ministry eschewing "false Calvinism" and sparking the dawn of the Modern Missions Movement.[16] There, in the Northamptonshire Association of Baptist Churches, he would meet the likes of John Ryland, Jr. of Northampton, John Sutcliffe of Olney, then Samuel Pearce of Birmingham and William Carey of Leicester. Fuller's famous relationship with Carey forged a now-legendary mission to India in which Fuller would "hold the rope" for Carey back in England. As to Samuel Pearce, Fuller regarded the pastor so highly that he wrote his *Memoirs of the Rev. Samuel Pearce* (1800) to serve as a paradigm for piety: "The governing principle in Mr. Pearce, beyond all doubt, was holy love ... his religion was that of the heart."[17] A century later, Samuel Pearce (1766–1799) was dubbed "the Baptist Brainerd" due to the strong correlation between the two men and their lives of spiritual devotion.[18]

Like Edwards, Fuller attempted only one biographical study, again prompting comparisons between the Connecticut River Puritan and the pastor from Kettering. According to Michael Haykin, it is important to note "Fuller's clear indebtedness to what is probably the most popular of the American divine's books, namely, his account of the life and ministry of David Brainerd (1718–1747)."[19] Fuller began work on the *Memoirs* not long after hearing of Pearce's death while on a fund-raising

[10] Haykin 2001, p. 27

[11] This was also the year that Fuller lost his first wife Sarah (Gardiner) Fuller.

[12] Fuller was baptized at Soham in 1770. Eve's homiletical model is sufficiently summarized in one short observation by Fuller: the pastor "had little or nothing to say to the unconverted." Eve subsequently left the church at Soham in 1771 over a controversy involving church discipline of a drunken church member. The issue involved the necessary consequences of a High Calvinistic piety.

[13] Matthew 28:19–20, for example, had become a favorite ecclesiological text within the Particular Baptist community, serving as the *locus classicus* for believer's baptism. Fuller also saw this text as a missiological one still in force.

[14] "The Modern Question" is one of seeming theological tension: Are sinners under obligation to repent and believe in the Gospel despite their sinful inability to believe?

[15] Fuller 1988, 2:329

[16] According to John Piper, the endeavors of Fuller and William Carey provided a prosperous period of evangelism (1793-1865) that constituted the first age in modern missions. Hudson Taylor's founding of the China Inland Mission in 1865 would initiate the second.

[17] Fuller 1988, 1:429

[18] Carey 1913

[19] Haykin, notes, p. 1

Fig. 6: Samuel Pearce (1766–99)

trip in Scotland for the Baptist Missionary Society. The news brought Fuller to tears . . . and action. The idea for Pearce's biography was not a new one, but the proper window and impetus had been supplied. Fuller desired to show the world a remarkable example of Christian spirituality and support Pearce's widow Sarah and her five children.[20] The end product would be a biography that paralleled Edwards's *Brainerd* in many ways, beginning with the very purpose for which it was written.

Men of Piety

The "seraphic Pearce" served as a paradigm for piety.[21] According to Fuller, "the great ends of Christian biography are instruction and example. By faithfully describing the lives of men eminent for godliness, we not only embalm their memory, but furnish ourselves with fresh materials and motives for a holy life."[22] Interestingly, similar language is employed at the beginning of Edwards's *Brainerd*:

> But notwithstanding all these imperfections, I am persuaded every pious and judicious reader will acknowledge, that what is here set before them is indeed a remarkable instance of true and eminent Christian piety in heart and practice—tending greatly to confirm the reality of vital religion, and the power of godliness—that it is most worthy of imitation, and many ways calculated to promote the spiritual benefit of the careful observer.[23]

For both theologians, the telos of biographical theology was godliness. Fuller's model of "instruction and example," as set forth in Pearce, parallels Edwards's model for "practice" and "imitation" in Brainerd. The purpose is the same. Fuller draws strongly from his predecessor's structure and language before the *Memoirs* even begin. What David Brainerd was able to achieve for Fuller in his own personal spirituality, Fuller is seeking to replicate through Pearce for the souls of his English community.

To classify either work as hagiography would miss its intention. Each features a man transparently in need of a Savior. In turn, seasons of unbelief for both men serve as the means through which they learned to exercise their faith and cling to Christ. In the words of Pearce, "A few seasons of spirituality I have enjoyed; but my heart, my inconstant heart, is too prone to rove from its proper centre."[24] In reality, Brainerd's internal struggles were not simply inspirational; they became integral for the way Pearce viewed his own suffering:

> Thinking that I might get some assistance from David Brainerd's experience, I read his life to the time of his being appointed a missionary among the Indians. The exalted devotion of that dear man almost made me question mine. Yet, at some seasons, he speaks of sinking as well

as rising. His singular piety excepted, his feelings, his prayers, desires, comforts, hopes, and sorrows are my own.[25]

[25] Fuller 1988, 1:376–77

Pearce clearly saw himself in Brainerd. The "sinking as well as rising" that Pearce mentions would have been mutually familiar to any reader of *Brainerd*, as the American missionary's seasons of depression were *sine qua non* with his spiritual journey.[26] Pearce himself did not seem to experience the same degree of melancholy as Brainerd, however, the piety of both men brought them to realize and embrace their spiritual valleys.

[26] According to Michael J. McClymond and Gerald R. McDermott, "Brainerd's self-denial and mortification was so extreme that it ruined his health and likely contributed to his premature death" (McClymond and McDermott, 2012, p. 63).

Several years after writing *Religious Affections* (1746) and beginning to write *The Life of David Brainerd*, Edwards began to view depression much more existentially. At twenty-nine, the young Brainerd had died in the pastor's Northampton home. Edwards had witnessed for himself the gloom of his dear friend's despondency.[27] Depression was now described as a "disease," a "melancholy" capable of producing "dark thoughts" of "spiritual desertion."[28] These experiences had brought Brainerd to describe himself in such a poor spiritual light that at times it appears as if the missionary questioned his own salvation. If the Apostle Paul was the "chief of sinners," Brainerd clearly self-identified as the archbishop! "I saw so much of my hellish vileness, that I appeared worse to myself than any devil: I wondered that God would let me live, and wondered that people did not stone me, much more that they would ever hear me preach!"[29] This was but a single episode in Brainerd's fluctuating psychological state. For this reason, Perry Miller has called Edwards's *David Brainerd* "a minor masterpiece of psychological confession."[30]

[27] Brainerd himself died in Edwards' home in 1747.

[28] Sermon 509 on Matt. 25:46 (*WJEO* 54)

[29] *WJE* 7:176

[30] Miller 2005, p. 246

Nevertheless, it is ultimately the missionary's crucicentrism that Edwards accentuates over his psychology. Brainerd's spiritual wilderness brought him (and Edwards) to savor the excellence and perfection of Christ all the more. Conrad Cherry effectively describes Edwards's perspective of these sufferings:

> No soul ever rose to higher spiritual peaks of delight only to descend into the lowest melancholia, than did Brainerd's. But Edwards' eye is upon the "principle," the "light," the "habit," which is not to be confused with psychological states of the saints. His vision is directed toward that abiding habit which persisted in, through, and behind the risings and fallings of Brainerd's spirits, toward that "great change" and "abiding change" wrought in conversion which abides as the saint's foundation but not as his controllable possession.[31]

Fig. 7: David Brainerd (1718–47)

[31] Cherry 1990, pp. 38–39

This kind of inner turmoil also showed itself in Pearce, who uses parallel language in his self-abasement: "I think I am the most vile, ungrateful servant that ever Jesus Christ employed in his church! At some times, I question whether I ever knew the grace of God in truth; and at others I hesitate on the most important points of Christian

[32] Fuller 1988, 3:401

[33] Such was also a result of indwelling sin yet to be extinguished in the midst of conforming to Christ. Pearce's doctrine of depravity is consistent with a Calvinistic hamartiology: "I am all sin; I cannot think, nor act, but every motion is sin." (Fuller, 1988, 3:401)

[34] Haykin 2001, p. 133

[35] Fuller 1988, 3:418. Fuller even describes Pearce in such a way: "Cheerfulness was as natural to him as breathing" (Fuller, 1988, 3:437).

[36] Murray 1987, p. 305

[37] WJE 7:91

[38] Fuller 1988, 3:445

faith."[32] Such raw introspection is rather shocking at times in both biographies. Yet these unfiltered expressions of spiritual deadness serve both as spiritual catharsis for the writer as well as spiritual therapy for the reader. For Fuller, this undulating journey toward holiness was consonant with the process of sanctification.[33] Seasons of sinfulness and stagnant faith were to be overcome, "not so much by maintaining a direction opposition to it, as by cultivating opposite principles."[34] Diary-keeping and Christian biography were Puritanical traditions of spiritual cultivation bequeathed to both Pearce and Fuller by Edwards through the godly medium of David Brainerd. Their principal aim was to joyfully draw near to the Lord, and spiritual valleys aided in looking to the glory of the cross. As a result, in the midst of trial Pearce could confidently speak of a joy "unspeakable and full of glory."[35]

Still another commonality between Samuel Pearce and David Brainerd was their mortal end. The cause of their deaths was the same: tuberculosis. Pearce died at the age of thirty-three of pulmonary tuberculosis after a steady bout with the deadly disease. Brainerd likewise suffered from tuberculosis and passed away in Edwards's home at the age of twenty-nine. Before their premature deaths, both young men endured and documented their prolonged illnesses. However, while the way in which these two men died was very similar, it was the *manner* in which they died that inspired their respective biographers. According to Iain Murray, "the presence of a dying man, through many weeks, was uplifting to Edwards."[36] The Northampton pastor cherished the privilege of witnessing "the effects of (Brainerd's) religion in dying circumstances."[37] Those effects galvanized Edwards into a biographic memorial of the man and his life. Decades later, Pearce's death brought Fuller to also consider the quantity and quality of human life. The impact of Christ's thirty-three years had been immeasurable, yet his death was the apex of a life lived unto the Father. Such was the way Fuller saw Pearce in his own death. The Birmingham pastor's humility and faith in the end were enough for Fuller to weigh the true significance of life: "There is undoubtedly a way of rendering a short life a long one, and a long life a short one, by filling or not filling it with proper materials. That time which is squandered away in sloth, or trifling pursuits, forms a kind of blank in human life."[38] This kind of reflection-exhortation is incredibly important for the very purpose Fuller penned *Memoirs of the Rev. Samuel Pearce, M.A.* Pearce was an example of evangelical piety, and Fuller aimed to motivate his readers to imitate Pearce's life of meaningful selflessness. That included evangelism. The Baptist Missionary Society stood to gain from Pearce's life of piety, and Fuller wished to capture it for others to enjoy.

The inspiration both men provided in their last days stemmed not simply from their irenic disposition in waiting for death, but also in their gleeful anticipation of it. Jonathan Edwards was pleased to witness Brainerd's hope firsthand in his own home: "He often used the epithet, *glorious,* when speaking of the day of his *death,* calling it that *glorious day* . . . and the nearer death approached, the more desirous he seemed to be of it."[39] Physical death was not simply the entrance into eternity. For Brainerd, imminent death became a means of further sanctification and Godward concentration. As George Marsden notes, "David Brainerd could endure his sufferings and impending death with profound tranquility because he so clearly saw reality in this cosmic context. Such a God-centered perspective enabled him to act as one who 'had indeed sold all for Christ.' "[40] The same Pauline excitement toward death can also be heard in Pearce in the midst of his own illness: "As to myself, I thank God that I am not without a desire to depart, and to be with Christ, which is far better."[41] Both young men demonstrated this "desire to depart." Illness and calamity were nothing more than preparation for glory. Fuller and Edwards both expend much of their biographies depicting the last months of their subjects, indicating that this was a significant part of the story they wished to tell. Perhaps nothing displayed Christian piety more than the passionate earthly exits of both men. Indeed, the ample space allotted to their final days is indicative of common authorial purpose, and Fuller's model clearly follows Edwards's. As Tom Nettles insightfully observes, "Intimate acquaintance with the ideas of a great theologian tends to make the student a wise and sensitive pastor. Fuller took the difficult ideas of Edwards, digested their spiritual implications and used them for the good of souls."[42] What the natural-moral inability distinction and religious sensibilities generated for Fuller's polemical soteriology, the piety of David Brainerd accomplished for Fuller's (and Pearce's) own spiritual devotion. And their shared brand of piety was an especially evangelical one.

Men of Evangelism

One prominent distinction between the two men was their vocations. Unlike David Brainerd, Samuel Pearce was *not* a missionary. He was the pastor of Cannon Street Baptist Church in Birmingham, England.[43] Pastoral duties, however, were not the supreme desire of Pearce's heart. He much longed to serve the Baptist Missionary Society as an international missionary. Pearce wrote to Carey expressing his excitement at this very prospect: "I should call that the happiest hour of my life which witnessed our *both* embarking with our families on board one ship, as helpers of the servants of Jesus Christ already in Hindostan."[44] Pearce's zeal for the Great Commission is palpable throughout the book. Fuller, the founding secretary of the Baptist

[39] *WJE* 7:464

[40] Marsden 2003, p. 327

[41] Fuller 1988, 3:415

[42] Nettles 2008, p. 127

[43] Pearce graduated from the well-known Bristol Baptist Academy.

[44] Fuller 1988, 3:380

Missionary Society, intended this missiological tone. However, Pearce invoked awe from Fuller not for his overseas endeavors, but for his faithfulness to the cause of Christ in the face of personal rejection. Samuel Pearce's dreams of becoming a missionary were never realized. Fuller even records the reasoning behind the mission committee's decision:

> The committee, after the most serious and mature deliberation, though they were fully satisfied as to brother Pearce's qualifications, and greatly approved of his spirit, yet were unanimously of opinion *that he ought not to go;* and that not merely on account of his connexions at home, which might have been pleaded in the case of brother Carey, but on account of the mission itself, which required his assistance in the station which he already occupied.[45]

Despite the unfortunate news of rejection, Pearce was unwavering in his Gospel exuberance.[46] The optimistic pastor wrote to his wife Sarah soon after the news and began simply, "I am disappointed, but not dismayed."[47] Such was an example of the reason Fuller admired Pearce: his belief in the sovereignty of God and his constant drive for the Great Commission. Both manifested most vividly in the face of adversity. Fuller writes, "The decision of the committee, though it rendered him much more reconciled to abide in his native country than he could have been without it, yet did not in the least abate his zeal for the object. As he could not promote it abroad, he seemed resolved to lay himself out more for it at home."[48] In Pearce's heart, he believed that God had kindly denied his request: "I have much confidence in the judgment of my brethren, and hope I shall be perfectly satisfied with their advice."[49] After learning of the committee's decision, Pearce did not quiet his rumblings; he simply learned to channel them constructively for the kingdom of God. For one such as Pearce, supreme love was to God and God alone.

A strong Calvinistic belief in the sovereignty of God is one of the strongest bonds conjoining David Brainerd and Samuel Pearce. For instance, Brainerd is incapable of speaking about the success of the Gospel without attributing full responsibility and power to God: "My whole dependence and hope of success seemed to be on God; who alone I saw could make them willing to receive instruction."[50] This high view of God's providence sustained both men not only in evangelism but in tragedy as well. Pearce, for example, carried a seemingly stoic disposition during the tragic loss of his daughter to illness.[51] Facing his own death, Brainerd exercised similar faith in God's complete and utter sovereignty over His creation: "Whether I should ever recover or no, seemed very doubtful; but this was many times a comfort to me, that *life* and *death* did not depend upon *my* choice."[52] All was God's and thus all was to be received from Him alone. This strong sense of

[45] Fuller 1988, 3:383

[46] Brainerd himself gladly submitted to his own ecclesial and extra-ecclesial authorities as if they were a word from God. Brainerd was examined by the Association at Danbury in order to receive his preaching license. He also took and passed an examination for ordination at a Newark Presbytery. Finally, Brainerd was examined in New York, New Jersey, and Pennsylvania by correspondents of the honourable 'Society in Scotland for the Propagating of Christian Knowledge.' Both Fuller and Brainerd were two zealous souls who still submitted to the proper channels of authorities in their lives. This quality in both men went much appreciated by their respective biographers.

[47] Fuller 1988, 3:383
[48] Fuller 1988, 3:384
[49] Fuller 1988, 3:393

[50] WJE 7:254

[51] On December 13, 1794, Pearce writes to his wife Sarah: "We must not, however, suffer ourselves to be infected with a mental fever on this account. Is she ill? It is right. Is she very ill ... dying? It is still right" (WJE 7:393).

[52] WJE 7:373

divine sovereignty, while shared by both authors, was especially strong in Andrew Fuller's household. Of the eleven children that Andrew Fuller fathered, eight died in infancy or early childhood.[53] Fuller no doubt shared in Pearce's suffering during this time.

Despite the trans-Atlantic gulf between them along with their different historical contexts, the strongest commonality between the two men was their greatest mutual desire: the Gospel. David Brainerd and Samuel Pearce worked their faith out practically in an especially evangelical piety that sought to save a condemned world. Consequently, the Great Commission was a text that both men saw as binding to the modern-day church. Samuel Pearce stood next to William Carey on the conviction that Matthew 28:19–20 was still in effect for Christians everywhere:

> I here referred to our Lord's commission, which I could not but consider as universal in its object and permanent in its obligations. I read brother Carey's remarks upon it; and as the command has never been repealed— as there are millions of beings in the world on whom the command may be exercised—as I can produce no counter-revelation—and as I lie under no natural impossibilities of performing it—I conclude that I, as a servant of Christ, was bound by this law.[54]

Pearce aligned himself with Carey *and* Fuller in this regard. In fact, Paul Brewster locates evangelism as the overarching theme of Fuller's ministry: "Fuller's greatest legacy among the Baptists: to support a missionary-oriented theology that helped foster deep concern for the salvation of the lost."[55] What better vessel to carry a vital message to the public than someone who embodied that very message! *Memoirs of the Rev. Samuel Pearce* packaged Fuller's invitational Calvinism in biographical form. In this way, Michael Haykin is correct when he states, "Memoirs are a sort of apologetic for the BMS' work in India – and evangelical activism, typical of eighteenth-century Evangelicalism (thus the mission to Ireland). But also he is presenting Pearce as a model of evangelical piety—one that is seen most purely in his dying days."[56]

At this point, some may be tempted to drive a wedge between Edwards's approach and Fuller's, assuming that the latter was more "mission-minded" in his biography. However this is an inaccurate assessment of Edwardsean theology. While Paul Brewster is correct in identifying Fuller's clear missiological legacy, this in no way negates the evangelical piety that Edwards means to convey in *The Life of David Brainerd*. While it may be conceded that Edwards's legacy has become a bit more "metaphysical" and "rational" in recent theological circles, the Puritan theologian's missiological purposes in *Brainerd* are undeniable.

To divorce Brainerd's spiritual devotion from his ministerial work is simply impossible. Edwards's high praise for Brainerd leaves little

[53] This is not to diminish in any way Edwards' doctrine of divine providence. He too had eleven children, of which ten actually lived to adulthood.

[54] Fuller 1988, 3:386

[55] Brewster 2010, p. 106

[56] Haykin, notes, p. 17

57 *WJE* 7:92

58 Bezzant 2014, p. 166

59 Conforti 1995, p. 3

60 McDermott 1995, pp. 258–73

61 Bezzant 2014, p. 149

62 *WJE* 7:256

63 *WJE* 7:437

question that his selection of a missionary for arguably his most popular work is beyond coincidence: "He had a talent for describing the various workings of this imaginary, enthusiastic religion—evincing its falseness and vanity, and demonstrating the great difference between this and true spiritual devotion—which I scarcely ever knew equaled in any person."[57] Brainerd's strength was found in his weakness. His authentic faith and evangelical piety were such that Rhys Bezzant maintains, "Edwards presents Brained as a man of great perseverance despite incapacity, prayer despite doubt, and self-sacrifice despite meager resources. Brainerd embodied generic evangelical piety."[58] Brainerd was an extraordinary, everyday sinner. Therefore, as made explicit at the beginning of his biography, Edwards wished for him to be imitated. A generation later, Fuller and Pearce found him worthy of imitation. Fuller's *Memoirs of the Rev. Samuel Pearce* confirms Joseph Conforti's assertion that Edwards passed down an "evangelical culture, which developed an American literature of its own modeled on such canonical works as Edwards's *Life of David Brainerd*."[59]

Therefore Fuller's evangelical biography has Edwards's as its prototype. Without question, Fuller would have been intimate not only with *Brainerd* but with Edwards's own missionary experience. Jonathan Edwards himself deployed to the mission field for seven years at Stockbridge (1751–1758), between his pastorate at Northampton and his short-lived presidency at the College of New Jersey. After his removal from Northampton, Edwards was offered at least two "comfortable pulpits in New England" in addition to ministerial positions in Scotland via his dear friend John Erskine.[60] In the end, he willfully chose to preach to the American Indians, similar to Brainerd. Edwards's postmillennialism was grounded in an extremely optimistic view of the success of the church and its cause. Consequently, Bezzant has called Edwards an "ecclesial internationalist."[61] The Connecticut River Puritan's expansive Great Commission pursuits provided much of the impetus for his *Life of David Brainerd*, a subject imbued with Edwardsean spirituality. David Brainerd was the missiology of Jonathan Edwards personified—a missiology inherited by the Baptist Missionary Society.

With an ocean and a generation between them, Brainerd and Pearce fixed their eyes upon the same target: the heathen. From an early age, Brainerd held a special place in his heart for the lost, and he pleaded with God to be sent on His behalf: "My great concern was for the conversion of the heathen to God; and the Lord helped me to plead with him for it."[62] Brainerd's theocentric focus was thoroughly Edwardsean, continually directed to the lost for the sake of God alone: "Oh that all people might love and praise the blessed God; that he might have all possible honour and glory from the intelligent world!"[63]

Likewise, Samuel Pearce, who fought off Antinomians in his own

Birmingham congregation, worked diligently to seek out those same heathen: "O how I love that man whose soul is deeply affected with the importance of the precious gospel to idolatrous heathens!"[64] Fuller portrays Pearce as a gregarious pastor—a humble servant of the Lord who delighted in the friendship of other believers. In the community of the church, Pearce found the intersection of God's greatest gifts and purposes. Therefore nothing defined true Christian friendship more than a common Commission and the evangelical piety derived from it: "The soul of Mr. Pearce was formed for friendship . . . the grand cement of his friendship was kindred piety."[65] In no uncertain terms, Fuller paints his pietistic motif through the medium of friendship, a fellowship of men who all embodied one singular cause: to fulfill Christ's last earthly command. The Northamptonshire Association became a group of commissioned men who not only nurtured Pearce's soul; they also introduced him to the very theologian who would hand him the piety of David Brainerd.

Likewise, in the mountains, Brainerd often traveled with close friends mutually invested in the work of the Gospel: "O how desirable it is, to keep company with God's dear children! These are the 'excellent ones of the earth in whom,' I can truly say, 'is all my delight.' "[66] Here we find yet another commonality between the two biographical protagonists. For both men, true friendship was centripetal around the Gospel and Christ's Great Commission. Fuller highlighted the gift of Christian friendship in the memoirs of Pearce, something he no doubt admired in the life of Brainerd.

A Particular Redemption

As pastor-theologian, Fuller's theology informed his homiletics. In his youth, under the High Calvinist scheme, the pastor at Soham had shied away from making second-person invitations for salvation. According to Fuller, since unregenerate sinners had no natural ability for faith, they were not under any obligation to perform duties that were physically impossible. Thus ministers were not under any obligation to preach a Gospel that their hearers could not naturally believe. Where there was no ability, there was no duty.[67] However, the entire system created problems in Fuller's mind. Over time, he began to sense his preaching was "anti-scriptural" and in need of prognosis. Around this time Robert Hall, pastor of the Particular Baptist Church in Arnesby, Leicestershire, suggested that he read Jonathan Edwards's classic work on the *Freedom of the Will*. Fuller immersed himself in the dense volume, along with those of John Bunyan and John Gill, in hopes of clarifying the minister's responsibility when preaching to men and women under the complete bondage of sin. The "Modern Question" begged to be

[64] Fuller 1988, 3:379

[65] Fuller 1988, 3:372

[66] *WJE* 7:296

[67] In this way, the High Calvinists had in some ways recapitulated the Arminian scheme.

answered: are sinners under obligation to repent and believe in the Gospel despite their inability to believe? After weighing the obvious differences between Bunyan and Gill, and with the help of Edwards, Fuller was able to finally answer the question with an affirmative. There was a clear duty. Thus he added an adequate, yet lengthy, subtitle to The *Gospel Worthy of All Acceptation: The Obligations of Men Fully to Credit, and Cordially to Approve, Whatever God Makes Known, Wherein is Considered the Nature of Faith in Christ, and the Duty of Those where the Gospel Comes in that Matter* (1785). The second edition, which appeared in 1801, was simply subtitled: *The Duty of Sinners to Believe in Jesus Christ.* As Edwards's distinction between natural and moral inability proved, one's theology will always dictate one's methodology, or more appropriately, one's missiology. Once Fuller was able to reconcile human responsibility and divine sovereignty, he was able to create a robust evangelical Calvinism that would galvanize the Modern Missions Movement.[68] However, *Freedom of the Will* wasn't the only work by Edwards that influenced Fuller's soteriology. His *Life of David Brainerd* presented an exemplary Christian model coupled with a practical evangelical theology.

In his *The Gospel Worthy of All Acceptation*, Fuller describes a nuanced doctrine of particular redemption. Christ's atonement, he posits, is "itself equal to the salvation of the whole world, were the whole world to embrace it—and the peculiarity which attends it consists not in its insufficiency to save more than are saved, but in the sovereignty of its application."[69] In short, God is sovereign over the efficacy of his own atoning sacrifice. The intrinsic worth of Christ's work on the cross is infinite because God Himself is infinite. So in this way, the atonement *can be* universal if God so deemed it. However, in its application the atonement *actually* suffices for the elect whose sins are effactually cleansed. This is Fuller's nuanced doctrine of particular redemption, holding that "(Christ) may apply his sacrifice to the salvation of some men, and not of others."[70] While Fuller has been accused of shrugging off definite atonement, his soteriological position remains thoroughly "particular" (as would be expected for a "Particular" Baptist). However, Fuller is neither completely "Reformed" in the classical sense, nor a General Baptist.[71] Despite the easy confusion for the modern Reformed mind, Jeremy Pittsley sees Edwardsean thought buttressing "Fullerism": "Edwards' understanding on moral vis-à-vis natural inability and his understanding of the infinite value of the atonement would ultimately unite in Fuller's view of the universal sufficiency of the atonement."[72] Thus in two biographies featuring missiologically-minded ministers (forgive the alliteration), it should also be understood that each author wished to present his own soteriological beliefs. Better still, both Brainerd and Pearce were men selected for exposition due to their

[68] Questions surrounding human epistemology were to be answered after belief in the Gospel, not while waiting for a 'warrant of faith.' One's election cannot be confirmed by anything else outside of faith itself.

[69] Fuller 1988, 3:374

[70] Fuller 1988, 3:374

[71] Fuller included substantial differences between the first and second editions of *The Gospel Worthy of All Acceptation*, relating to the doctrine of particular redemption. Fuller seemed to endorse a more governmental theory of the atonement, and some accused him of relinquishing the doctrine of penal substitution. Fuller of course faced substantial criticism for his first edition from Arminians like General Baptist Dan Taylor on one hand and High Calvinists like London Baptist pastors William Button and John Martin on the other. All of this fierce criticism took its toll on Fuller, however, this discussion proceeds outside the bounds of this paper.

[72] Pittsley 2008, p. 142

highly agreeable evangelical theology. Theology fuels missiology.

So what would Fuller find in Brainerd's life that would accord with his own nuanced doctrine of particular redemption? The answer is: much in fact. *The Life of David Brainerd* was more than a nice story about a nice person; it was a depiction of a man whose theology and missiology were perfectly congruent. In his exegesis of John 1:29, Brainerd explains its meaning: "And he is said to take away the sin of the world, not because all the world shall actually be redeemed from sin by him; but because, (1.) He has done and suffered sufficient to answer for the sins of the world, and so to redeem all mankind. (2.) He *actually* does take away the sins of the elect world."[73] For Edwards and Brainerd, Calvinism and evangelism were reconciled inside of this soteriological matrix. Furthermore, Brainerd's words are so near to those of Fuller that a theological correlation is incontrovertible. The pastor from Kettering adopted this same brand of sufficient-efficient atonement, and this in turn gave impetus to Fuller's fiercely missional theology.

Owing to Fuller and Pearce's familiarity with the lives and ministry of Edwards and Brainerd, the four men appear as links in a successive, historical chain. As a result, when Pearce's own language is examined, Jonathan Edwards himself can be heard. The Birmingham pastor's description of conversion is reminiscent of the Northampton pastor. In it we hear not only Edwardsean vocabulary but his pneumatology as well: "Now the Spirit hath revealed God in the Bible; but to an unbeliever the Bible is a sealed book. He can know nothing from a book that he looks upon as an imposture, and yet there is no other book in which God is revealed: so that to reject the Bible is to immerse ourselves in darkness, and, whilst professing to be wise, actually to become fools: whereas no sooner do we believe what the Spirit saith, than to us is God revealed, and in his light do we see light."[74] Pearce captures a thoroughly Reformed epistemology when he dichotomizes wisdom and foolishness, darkness and light. To him, supernatural revelation itself was the only means by which sinners are rescued from their spiritual blindness.[75] On the other hand, human responsibility and divine sovereignty are wrapped neatly into the same conversion. Pearce uses active words such as "reject" or "believe" while also maintaining that God must be passively "revealed." Like Fuller, Pearce believed that true election, or revelation of God, is introduced only when we "believe what the Spirit saith." There are no Gnostic undertones in Pearce's voluntaristic message of salvation. To a High Calvinist, such a description of conversion reeked of Arminianism. To Fuller, it was the quintessential paradigm of evangelical piety.

Pressing our ears against the words of Pearce, we can surely hear Edwards.[76] Chris Chun explains why the motif of light is an instant

[73] WJE 7:432

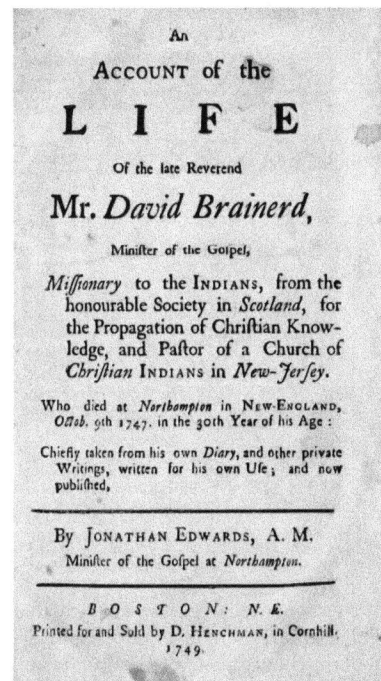

An
ACCOUNT of the
L I F E
Of the late Reverend
Mr. *David Brainerd*,
Minifter of the Goſpel,

Miſſionary to the INDIANS, from the honourable Society in *Scotland*, for the Propagation of Chriſtian Knowledge, and Paſtor of a Church of Chriſtian INDIANS in *New-Jerſey*.

Who died at *Northampton* in NEW-ENGLAND, *Octob.* 9th 1747. in the 30th Year of his Age:

Chiefly taken from his own *Diary*, and other private Writings, written for his own Uſe; and now publiſhed,

By JONATHAN EDWARDS, A. M.
Minifter of the Goſpel at *Northampton.*

B O S T O N: N. E.
Printed for and Sold by D. HENCHMAN, in Cornhill,
1749.

Fig. 8: Title page of *The Life of David Brainerd*

[74] Fuller 1988, 3:405

[75] Pearce's epistemology is consonant with Fuller's. In 1800 Fuller published *The Gospel Its Own Witness*, the definitive eighteenth-century Baptist response to the Deism of Thomas Paine. This work upheld the necessity of supernatural revelation unto salvation.

[76] Edwards' sermon "A Divine Supernatural Light" summarized the pneumatological epistemology found in his *Religious Affections.*

[77] Chun 2008, p. 121

[78] McClymond 1998, pp. 17–18

[79] Fuller 1988, 3:385

[80] Fuller 1988, 3:430

[81] This is not to suggest in any way that Fuller did not hold to a comprehensively Reformed doctrine of predestination and election.
[82] Fuller 1988, 3:430

[83] Fuller 1988, 3:431

[84] WJE 7:257
[85] WJE 7:288

clue to tracing Edwardsean pneumatological epistemology: "Among all the sensory perceptions, Edwards especially accentuates those that respond to metaphors of light and sight. The divine light is God's supernatural means by which perceiving human agents come to appreciate the beauty inherent within their faculties."[77] Michael McClymond dissects Edwardsean perception into three distinct categories, one of which includes light: "The *content* of perception is divine or spiritual 'excellency' or 'beauty'. The *mode* of perception is the 'divine light,' operating in and alongside the natural human faculties. The *sensibility* of perception is the 'spiritual sense' or 'new sense,' whose essence is 'delight' in God."[78] The light of the Holy Spirit penetrates into the darkest depths of the human soul to illumine divine glory in a "new sense" that characterizes the conversion experience. Adopting similar language, Pearce likens Christian converts to small lights who serve to further illumine the greatest Light: "Suitable frames of soul are like good lights, in which a painting appears to its full advantage."[79] Looking back upon the pious pastor's life, Fuller cannot help but see Pearce's illuminating influence upon his friends: his "constant aim (was) to promote the highest degrees of piety in himself and others."[80] The man who saw himself as the chief of sinners was remembered as one of the greatest, completely suiting Fuller's paradigm of piety. He truly was a "good light" to the world.

Theology fuels missiology. The sufficient-efficient system of atonement shared by both Brainerd and Pearce allowed for their vigorous evangelistic ministries unhindered by the chains of High Calvinism. Shrugging off the misinformed religion of John Eve, Fuller was able to personally invite sinners to faith instead of simply presenting a third-person narrative of the elect.[81] This harmonized well with Fuller's intense cruicentrism. According to Fuller of Pearce, "Christ crucified was his darling theme, from first to last."[82] According to Pearce, Christianity was a religion of crucifixion: "Now I see the value of the religion of the cross. It is a religion for a dying sinner. It is all the most guilty and the most wretched can desire."[83] Equipped with a brand of particular redemption that allowed for a free, sincere invitation to all, Fuller could now invite, plead, command, and urge sinners to believe in a Gospel for all. When the Scriptures revealed that the Lamb of God took away the sins of the world, Fuller could read it aloud without any hesitation or hermeneutical gymnastics. It is precisely this kind of invitational Calvinism that Brainerd handed Fuller and Pearce. Just a casual reading of Edwards's work reveals a man who employed the same kind of evangelical theology. With his thoughts ever on the heathen, Brainerd insists, "God helped me to plead with them, to 'turn from all the vanities of the heathen, to the living God."[84] He goes on: "I was enabled earnestly to invite the children of God to come renewedly."[85]

Edwards's Brainerd was an ocean apart from the High Calvinists of eighteenth-century England, literally and theologically. He pled. He invited. Furthermore, he evangelized with the same sincere theology crafted by Fuller years later, suggesting a strong correlation between Edwards and his early eighteenth-century counterpart. Edwardsean theology handed Fuller the necessary tools for an evangelical theology that would become the foundation for The Particular Baptist Society for Propagating the Gospel Among the Heathen. While the name may have needed doctoring, its soteriology was sufficiently Calvinistic *and* evangelistic.

Conclusion

Tom Nettles provides keen insight into the true depths of Edwards's influence upon Andrew Fuller's world: "Fuller and his entire circle of friends found within Jonathan Edwards the key to a peculiar theological perplexity that vexed their souls and virtually the entire Particular Baptist fellowship."[86] The faith and reason of the "public theologian" had emigrated from Northampton, Massachusetts to Fuller's Northamptonshire Association, re-shaping the Great Commission for its late eighteenth-century context.[87] The role that Edwards's *Life of David Brainerd* played in achieving this is never more evident than in Andrew Fuller's *Memoirs of the Rev. Samuel Pearce, M.A.* The piety, evangelism, and the definite atonement displayed in the respective biographies correspond to such a degree as to leave little doubt of Edwardsean influence upon the thought of Andrew Fuller. Through the spiritual parity between Samuel Pearce and David Brainerd, Jonathan Edwards should be invoked as a genuine inspiration to the Modern Missions Movement.

[86] Nettles 2008, p. 97

[87] Cherry 1990, p. xxiv

Jonathan Edwards and the Silkworm: Preaching and Typology

MATTHEW EVERHARD

In his memorable notebook, "Images of Divine Things," Jonathan Edwards draws a shocking parallel between the lowly silkworm and the Lord Jesus Christ. At first blush, the comparison is almost upsetting. But whereas most people would see a humble worm as a creature of significant disgust, Edwards saw a radiant reflection of God's work in redemption through the life, death, and resurrection of Jesus. He wrote,

> The silkworm is a remarkable type of Christ, which, when it dies, yields us that of which we make such glorious clothing. Christ became a worm for our sakes, and by his death finished that righteousness with which believers are clothed, and thereby procured that we should be clothed with robes of glory ... See II Sam. 5:23–24 and Ps. 84:6; the valley of mulberry trees.[1]

Well, there you have it: contemplating a wriggling worm should be a portal for godly minds by which we may view the redeeming glory of the Lord Jesus Christ! Right? Edwards explains how all of this works when he reasons, "Why should we not suppose that [God] makes the inferior in imitation of the superior, the material of the spiritual, on purpose to have a resemblance and shadow of them?"[2] He continues, "We see that even in the material world God makes one part of it strangely to agree with another; and why is it not reasonable to suppose he makes the whole as a shadow of the spiritual world?"[3] In fact, what Edwards does in this notebook he does similarly in his work of biblical theology, *The History of the Work of Redemption*. In this great series of sermons, which would have become his *magnum opus* (if he had lived long enough to complete it), one of his major goals was to show how all of the main elements of the Old Testament pointed to their reality in the fulfillment of the Gospel.[4]

What Edwards is describing here is called "typology," and when done correctly (as we shall later see) it is a legitimate way to view and

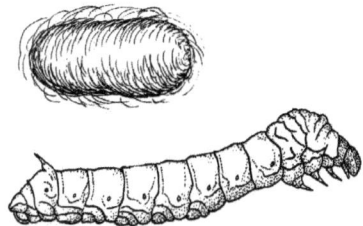

Fig. 9: A silkworm

[1] *WJE* 11:59

[2] *WJE* 11:53

[3] *WJE* 11:53

[4] See for instance *A History of the Work of Redemption* (*WJE* 9:204).

interpret the Bible. But Edwards would have us believe that typology goes even further and deeper still. Like the rabbit hole in *Alice in Wonderland,* Edwards saw the whole of creation as a means of sublime transport, preparing believers to view an entirely new realm of glory through the lens of the ordinary. In this way, Edwards saw the waves of the ocean as harbingers of the wrath of God, a man walking up a hill as an image of the saint's progress in sanctification, ravens feasting upon dead carcasses as the wicked acts of demonic spirits, and even bread-corn as a promise of resurrection glory.

Creative preachers who have the audacity to use typology in their sermons will sustain two distinct advantages. First, like Edwards, their sermons can be enhanced through the vivid employment of bold imagery such as that which the Northampton Puritan utilized in his silkworm comparison. By viewing the whole of the created order with new eyes, so to speak, one's preaching oratory can be opened up with new images, symbols, analogies, and illustrations virtually everywhere. This will greatly serve a preacher's use, especially in illustration and application. But secondly, and more importantly, the preacher's interpretation of the Bible itself will be enhanced and sharpened, assuming he uses typology correctly. This is true because Scripture itself explicitly utilizes typology—to a somewhat limited extent—in order to view many of its significant persons, places, and things, (especially in the Old Testament), through a Christological lens. In practice, this has the glorious effect of helping us to interpret our Bibles with a redemptive-historic purview in mind. But, as I just mentioned, the Bible does this in a *somewhat limited way* when compared to Edwards's comprehensive and extended use of typology almost everywhere. In what follows, we will explore this second function, that is, how using biblical typology correctly can actually improve our interpretation and our preaching as we seek to exegete the Scriptures more faithfully.

The Problem in Past Approaches: Establishing the Limits of Typology

Before going much further, we should probably give a sharper definition of what we mean by "types" and "typology." If we are not careful, this kind of interpretation can lead us into the wild and over-imaginative speculations that drew many to unrestrained methods of allegorical preaching, so common in ancient and medieval churches before the Reformation.[5] First, I will attempt my own definition of typology, and then I will quote some other scholars to help fill out our understanding. I define a type as an image or symbol most often (but not always) found in the Old Testament, rich with redemptive-historical significance, and used with Biblical warrant, to better illustrate the

[5] See Sidney Greidanus's very helpful exploration of the history of allegorical preaching (Greidanus, 1999, pp. 70–90).

Gospel. Thus, a type is combined or linked with an antitype which corresponds to its fulfillment. A very obvious example is the way in which the Old Testament sacrifices prefigured the glorious atonement brought about by Jesus Christ's ultimate sacrifice on the cross. This is of course a major theme of the book of Hebrews, and as such, the type/antitype connection is entirely warranted. Sidney Greidanus tells us that this differs from allegory in that allegory is not necessarily as attuned to the unfolding drama of biblical redemption as a type would necessarily be. Thus Greidanus defines typology as "the search for linkages between events, persons, or things *within the framework of revelation*, whereas allegorism is the search for secondary and hidden meaning underlying the primary and obvious meaning of a narrative" (emphasis in original).[6] I also like the colloquial definition given by David Murray; he calls typology "picture-ology,"[7] since types tend to hold significant theological truths in vivid image.

[6] Greidanus 1999, p. 91

[7] Murray 2013, p. 136

Greener readers of the Bible may not be familiar with typology as an interpretive tool, and your average small group Bible study probably never touches on this topic at all during open discussion. Having grown up in evangelical, Bible-preaching churches for most of my life, I cannot remember hearing many sermons (if any) that employed this term or even used the concept as a way to explain Scripture to common believers in the pews. Most modern preaching, so heavy on moralistic lecturing ("Do this! Don't do that!") and life application sermonizing ("Ten easy steps to a better marriage!") probably tread far too lightly on the great pictures and images of the Old Testament which foretell the glories of redemption. This may be a problem somewhat unique to our age, since previous generations flew the other direction entirely on the continuum, preferring sermons rich with allegory, that went far beyond a bald reading and application of the text. Greidanus tells us that from the third to sixteenth centuries, allegory was the predominant method of preaching.[8] So, it seems that while our own generation is mostly unaware of the existence of typology, especially in the Old Testament, previous generations bent it much too far, attempting to see multiple contorted layers of meaning in any given text. Not only that, but the absence of typology from one's hermeneutical repertoire may lead the reader or preacher to make disastrous errors. Dispensationalism, for instance, usually demands and requires a literal fulfillment to what may be merely biblical types, ironically detracting from a passage its intended redemptive fulfillment by substituting a rigid literalism. A dispensationalist may insist, for instance, that land grants to Israel must be fulfilled literally and exactly sometime in the future. Not only that, but he certainly expects the reconstitution of a literal temple, and some even anticipate a return to animal sacrifices! Goldsworthy thinks this type of over-literalism is an error which typology helps to correct:

[8] Greidanus 1999, p. 70

[9] Goldsworthy 1991, p. 68

"Typology, then, takes account of the fact that God used a particular part of human history to reveal himself and his purposes to mankind. But it was a process, so that the historical types are incomplete revelations and depend on their antitype for their real meaning. Typology rejects the principle of literalism."[9]

There can be no doubt that the Bible itself uses typology, recommending such an interpretative grid to us in the works of the canonical writers themselves. Paul tells us that "Death reigned from Adam to Moses, even over those whose sinning was not like the transgression of Adam, *who was a type of the one who was to come*" (Romans 5:14 ESV, emphasis added). Thus he connects Adam to the Second Adam, the Lord Jesus Christ who obeyed where the first Adam failed in the Garden. The writer of Hebrews too, speaks of the tabernacle in the wilderness as portending far more significance than a mere tent in which the Israelites worshipped. He says, *"They serve a copy and shadow of the heavenly things. For when Moses was about to erect the tent, he was instructed by God, saying, 'See that you make everything according to the pattern that was shown you on the mountain'"* (Hebrews 8:5 ESV, emphasis added). So too, later in the same book, the author indicates that the Law itself was "but a shadow of the good things to come instead of the true form of these realities" (Hebrews 10:1 ESV). In Colossians 2:16–17, Paul says, "Therefore let no one pass judgment on you in questions of food and drink, or with regard to a festival or a new moon or a Sabbath. These are a *shadow* of the things to come, but the substance belongs to Christ" (emphasis added). Other obvious usages of typology in the Scriptures include: Paul's assertion that the rock was a type of Christ (1 Corinthians 10:4), pervasive use of David as a type of Christ in relation to His messianic kingship (cf. Ezekiel 34:23), the temple as a type of the Church (Ephesians 2:21), the ark as a type of redemption through covenantal promise (1 Peter 3:20), and animal sacrifices as types of the atonement rendered through the blood of the cross (Hebrews 9:23).

The Cause of Difficulty: Imaginative Hermeneutics

So the Bible warrants typology, that is to say, the drawing of direct lines of comparison between a sign or symbol with its greater fulfillment, corresponding with God's purposes in redemption history. Nevertheless, the salient questions we must face are "How far can we take this?" And, "Where does it end?" For instance, can we positively connect with any biblical warrant that the fact that Esau was a hairy man (Genesis 25:25) with the "righteousness that is by faith" (Romans 1:17)? Probably not. Scripture never makes that connection explicitly, and it would seem to be drawn entirely from the imagination of the reader. Or can we suggest overtly that the gopher wood from which the ark was constructed was a sure type of the wooden cross of Calvary? Unlikely. These sorts of suggestions may be creative and attractive to a preacher who is eager to move quickly from the Old Testament to the New Testament, but are also dangerously innovative. Rather, they draw the listener unnecessarily into the realm of the preacher's creative speculation. Bryan Chapell calls this "leapfrogging," and dissuades preachers from attempting such homiletical moves.[10] Unfortunately, these slippery exegetical moves in the study are sometimes received as being nearly ingenious by the audiences of many incautious preachers. John Chrysostom warned of this danger when he wrote that, "The practice of importing into Holy Scripture alien ideas of one's own imagination instead of accepting what stands written in the text, in my opinion, carries great danger for those who have the hardihood to follow it."[11]

[10] Chapell 1994, p. 294

[11] Greidanus 1999, pp. 94–95

In a very helpful section on the strengths and weakness of typology, Sidney Greidanus warns readers that using types too imaginatively can very precipitously lead exegetes and preachers into the kind of speculation that is unwarranted from the text itself. In this way, the exegete takes a source person, place, or object, merely incidental to the text, and creates his own bridge to a New Testament fulfillment that may or may not have any overt Biblical connection. Greidanus names Justin Martyr and Irenaeus as egregious violators of an overly imaginative symbol mapping. Historical examples of this might include comparing the fact that Eve was made from Adam's side (for instance) to the spear being driven into Jesus' side on the cross. In these cases, the type/antitype agreement is largely arbitrary. Modern day preachers would do well to avoid the excessive creativity required for this type of leap.

Jonathan Edwards, despite his proclivity towards seeing types ubiquitously in the natural world, gives some guidance that is very helpful in his *History of the Work of Redemption* as it regards finding types in the Bible.[12] There, he limits types of Christ in Scripture to three general kinds: 1) Instituted types. These are requirements of a legal or ceremonial kind that are fulfilled through the atonement of Jesus. Among them are the various kinds of sacrifices and aspects of tabernacle/temple worship. 2) Providential types. These are the great actions of God on behalf of His people that are recapitulated in the life, death, and resurrection of Jesus. Here we would include great events like the flood, the Passover, and the exile. Jesus fulfills these by becoming a greater conveyance of eternal deliverance than these temporal events in the time of Israel's history. 3) Personal types. These are most often carried out in the offices of Christ, as for instance in the typical Reformed designations of prophet, priest, and king. In this way, Christ is for God's people at once the great revealer of truth, the priestly atoner of

[12] *WJE* 9:204

our sins, and the one who rules on the throne of the Kingdom.

But did Edwards always follow his own rules? That question is certainly open for debate. If we are to take his work "Images of Divine Things" as our starting point for discussion, we would have to say, no. *Images* contains a vast array of types, going far beyond Scripture to nature, history, and science, having no explicit Old Testament/New Testament connection. Those types that Edwards saw and interpreted outside of the Biblical canon would certainly not meet his own three-fold standard. It would be hard to show from Scripture, for instance, how "gravity" corresponds to "love" (Image no. 79) or how the "late invention of the telescope" corresponds to the "great increase in the knowledge of heavenly things" which Edwards expected in his post-millennial view (Image no. 146).[13] But remember: in Edwards's unique understanding of the ubiquity of Gospel types, he is not making explicit exegetical claims here about the interpretation of Scripture. Thus, his threefold categorization of biblical types does not seem to apply to those extensive types he saw in the fields, barns, spider webs, and clear evening skies over Northampton. In this sense, it is almost as though Edwards has two great classifications of types: (1) those Biblical types that must correspond to his three categories named above, and (2) those types that transcend the Scriptures themselves, being encoded into the very fabric of the universe itself.

[13] *WJE* 11:81, 101

Contributions of the Redemptive Approach

But the fact that typology can be a slippery slope does not mean that it should be ruled out as an interpretive form. In fact, it greatly benefits our preaching by helping our people to see how some of the mysteries of the OT are revealed in Jesus. This has the benefit of making the OT a far more winsome book to read and study, as David Murray does in his *Jesus on Every Page*. As we have already stated, the canonical writers themselves interpret some OT passages typologically, opening a door through which we too may cautiously step. In fact, there are some distinct advantages to doing so. Let me name a couple of these homiletical benefits.

First, typology recognizes the progressive nature of revelation. This hermeneutical tool fully acknowledges that the work of redemption was not complete until the unfolding of the Christ Event, that is, the accomplishment of the redemption of God's elect through the life, death, and resurrection of Jesus Christ. Edwards would certainly agree with the progressive nature of revelation. This means that all along, God was moving history in a purposeful direction, superintending the unfolding of redemptive drama in such a way that it culminates in the events of Calvary. In this way, we can see how many of the things that occurred in the Old Testament were meant to prepare God's people for something much greater and fuller. That Jesus Christ "tabernacled among us" is not only a literal reading of John 1:14 in the Greek, it is also a correct use of typology: the tabernacle in the wilderness prepared the people of God to meet the God-man who came "enfleshed" in human form. Not only that, but through the use of typology, we can see how many of the great acts of God in the Old Testament can picture the redemptive work of Christ as it would eventually be fulfilled in due time.

The Passover for instance, can be regarded as a great type of the redemption of Christ as He delivers His own people out of slavery and into the promised land of grace, forgiveness, and the realization of God's new covenant. In fact, Paul explicitly connects Christ to the Passover Lamb in 1 Corinthians 5:7, another clear biblical use of typology. In this way, we can see many of the persons, places, and things of the OT as shadows indicating that a greater reality was yet to come in the Messianic Kingdom. Goldsworthy says, "Typology sees the type as part of the theological process of revelation that leads to the antitype or fulfillment in the gospel. The type is a shadow of the reality to be revealed in the antitype, but it is not a mere shadow."[14]

[14] Goldsworthy 1991, p. 77

But secondly, in terms of preaching itself, typological interpretation can help us to prevent what Bryan Chapell calls the "Deadly Be's."[15] These are sermons that are heavy laden with such themes as "Be more disciplined . . . ," "Be like David . . . ," and "Be good!"[16] In other words, our sermons should go beyond telling our people to try harder. Instead, they should be filled with the good news of Jesus Christ. In one example, we might compare two different ways to preach the story of Abraham's willing sacrifice of Isaac. A preacher who employs the "Deadly Be's" uses the text merely as an admonition towards ethical obedience. Here, the preacher teaches the story of Genesis 22, by making such applications as "See how strong Abraham's faith was? Why isn't your faith that strong? You need to have a faith that is as strong as Abraham's!" Although I am caricaturing a bit, we can see how a sermon like this would actually make an audience feel guiltier. The hearer beats herself up as she realizes that she could never do what Abraham was willing to do. But on the other hand, the preacher who approaches this text with a typological view in mind might see this as a type that is fulfilled in a greater way. Here, we can see God the Father being willing to offer His only Son on the cross for us. In this way, the preacher reminds the congregation that God was willing to do what He did not (ultimately) require Abraham to follow through with in Isaac. Not only does Abraham point as a type towards our perfect Heavenly Father's giving of His Son, but the ram offered in the place of Isaac can also be viewed as a type of substitutionary sacrifice, again fulfilled in antitype by Jesus. In this way, the preacher beckons the congregation

[15] Chapell 1994, pp. 281–84

[16] The problem with this, as Chapell says, is that "Be messages full only of moral instruction imply that we are able to change our fallen condition on our own strength. Such sermons communicate (although usually unintentionally) that we can clear the path to grace and that our works earn and/or secure our acceptance with God" (Chapell, 1994, p. 284).

to place their faith in the God who loves us enough to give His Son as a sacrifice for our sins. Overall, we see a much stronger Gospel sermon developing with the use of typology.

A More Profitable Approach in Light of a Christ-Centered Homiletic

So how can a preacher safely use typology to enliven his preaching of the Old Testament in order to faithfully move to Gospel implications? Bryan Chapell shows us the safest route: "Where New Testament writers specifically cite how an Old Testament person or feature prefigures the person and work of Christ—as with Adam, David, Melchizedek, the Passover, and the temple—the preacher may already safely use typological exposition."[17] I think that reading Edwards's works on types contained in Volume 11 of the Yale works helps us to think this way more and more. And that is a good thing. A Christian interpreter of the Old Testament, should come to any given passage longing to see how it promises the coming of the Messiah. No doubt, where the New Testament makes these connections explicit, so too may the modern preacher. He should not fear to do so. In fact, he must! In that way, preachers are doing what the text permits us to do, and even what the text *requires* us to do. This is the safest way to employ typology, and it does prevent us from possible exegetical error.

Bryan Chapell also gives us a good example of when to be a bit more cautious. In short, where no such fulfillment is explained in antitype by the NT, preachers should see an unavoidable "yield" sign in the road. Suppose the preacher wants to use Rahab's red cloth as a type of Christ (Joshua 2:21). Is this warranted by the text? Not explicitly, no. In that case, the preacher would have to invent an antitype that is not in the context to determine its fulfillment. We have no idea: Is the red cloth a type of the blood of Christ? Or is it the scarlet of our sins? We don't know, and perhaps that is because there is no Biblically warranted antitype at all. In cases like this, we should not feel free to invent an antitype out of thin air. Instances like these should produce extreme caution in the heart of the preacher about employing typology.

Overall, Goldsworthy is probably correct when he writes on the subject:

> Typology has been a somewhat controversial subject, possibly because of the strange excesses proposed by certain exponents of the method. But it is clearly a method based in the Scriptures themselves, and it cannot be ignored. Rightly understood, it opens up the structure of revelation in such a way that does not leave the connections to chance or imaginative thinking.[18]

So what can we say about Jonathan Edwards and his famous silkworm? Was he in error by creating such an elaborate notebook as

[17] Chapell 1994, p. 274

[18] Goldsworthy 1991, p. 76

"Images of Divine Things," filled with postulations about the spiritual meaning of thread-spinning invertebrates? Well, if he was merely examining the intricacies and glories of creation to see Christ in all things for the sake of his own devotional prayer life, probably not. But, on the other hand, if he were to preach such fanciful sermonic flourishes as authoritative from the pulpit of the Northampton Church with the same kind of certainty, he would probably do much better to just stay safely within his own threefold restrictions for typology which he himself lays down in *History of Redemption*. And while "Images of Divine Things" certainly does not lack creativity when it comes to Edwards's private notebooks on the natural world, the progress of science, and the unfolding of history, thankfully Edwards was far more cautious when bringing these ideas into the pulpit. So far as I can tell, Edwards used his overactive imagination with a respectable and admirable restraint when preaching: he allowed his extra-biblical types to color his sermons with vivid imagery (as, for example, in his most famous sermon *Sinners in the Hands of an Angry God*), but rarely, if ever, stretched a Biblical type beyond its exegetical warrant.

Jonathan Edwards and the Relationship between Habit and Practice in Christian Experience

DAVID LUKE

In a 1739 sermon on Hebrews 5:12 entitled, 'Every Christian should make a business of endeavouring to grow in knowledge of Divinity,' Edwards wrote approvingly that, 'divinity is commonly defined, *the doctrine of living to God*, and by some who seem to be more accurate, *the doctrine of living to God by Christ.*'[1] He went on to distinguish between the speculative or natural knowledge and the *practical* or *spiritual* knowledge of divinity.[2] While the former remained only in the head and affected no other faculty, the latter was a matter of the heart and affected heart, mind and will, and so resulted in action. Edwards was firmly rooted in a tradition where theology was an eminently practical subject.

Edwards's view that theology and practice went together belonged not only to the tradition that he inherited, but was also built into his view of the nature of the operations of the Holy Spirit in a person's life. Edwards, in keeping with the Reformed tradition, believed in the idea of the infusion of the Holy Spirit prior to the first act of faith. This infusion laid a new habit, principle or disposition in the soul (he uses the terms interchangeably). It was this new habit that was the source of holy living. Edwards described this habit, like all habits, as being,

> a law that God has fixed, that such actions upon such occasions should be exerted, the first new thing that there can be in the creature must be some actual alteration. So in the first birth it seems to me probable that the beginning of the existence of the soul, whose essence consists in powers and habits, is with some kind of new alteration there, either in motion or sensation.[3]

This essay explores the relationship between habit and practice in Edwards's thought, demonstrating that his emphasis on practice was fundamentally linked to his understanding of the role of habit. It begins

[1] *WJE* 22:86. This is language borrowed from Petrus Van Mastricht who it seems was following William Ames who defined theology as, 'the doctrine or teaching of living to God.' Ames was following his Cambridge tutor William Perkins who defined theology as 'the science of living blessedly for ever.'

[2] *WJE* 22:87.

Fig. 10: Petrus Van Mastricht (1630–1706)

[3] "Miscellany" no. 241, (*WJE* 13:358)

by exploring the place of habit in Reformed theology before considering Edwards's relationship with that tradition and how this worked itself out in his view of practice.

The Concept of Habit in Reformed Theology

For those in the Reformed Scholastic tradition, as Richard Muller writes, 'a faculty cannot receive a datum or act in a manner for which it has no capacity.'[4] In order for a person to have a capacity to receive a datum they needed a *habitus* (habit) or disposition to receive it. With regard to the gospel, this raised the issue of how it was possible for a person to respond in faith to the gospel if they lacked that habitus that had been lost at the Fall. To be able to respond to the gospel, Reformed Scholastics believed that a person must first receive a new habit from God. They essentially argued that prior to conversion God infuses the *habitus fidei*—the disposition of faith. Muller notes that this 'disposition, or habitus, is a potency for faith that can be actualized as faith.'[5] Despite some differences in understanding and emphasis, this idea was common amongst Reformed theologians where 'it became accepted that by regeneration, human beings receive a new nature which includes the power of faith that fallen man has lost by sin.'[6]

[5] Muller 1985, p. 22

[6] Wisse 2003, p. 203

Keen to protect against any suggestion that this *habitus fidei* was a source of merit, those who followed in the Reformed tradition of *sola fide* were careful to distinguish the *habitus fidei* from *iustitia infusa*—infused righteousness. The *habitus fide* and the correlated concept of *habitus gratiae*—disposition of grace—do not relate to inherent righteousness with regard to justification, but correspond to the work of the Holy Spirit in affecting the ability to exercise faith.[7]

[7] See Muller (Muller, 1985, p. 22) for a fuller discussion of the relationship between these terms.

This habit was not, however, considered as merely naked potential. Within the Reformed tradition it was believed that *habitus* would give rise to *actus*. Alexander Comrie (1706–1774) wrote that *habitus fidei* was 'wrought in the elect by the Holy Ghost with re-creating and irresistible power, when they are incorporated into Christ; by which they receive all the impressions which God the Holy Ghost imparts unto them through the Word.'[8] For Comrie, the act of faith was completely dependent upon the habit and the habit must necessarily give rise to the act. As Joel Beeke notes, Comrie found support for this position in the historic Protestant confessions and 'regarded the habitus of faith as the focus of historic Protestantism.'[9]

[8] Quoted in (Beeke, 1999, p. 218)

[9] Beeke 1999, p. 218

When it comes to Edwards, Norman Fiering says that his ideas on the subject of habit 'were relatively conventional, although much about the theory of habit was controversial, and there were opposing schools of thought.'[10] Fiering outlines this conventional view of habit as represented by such influential figures in Edwards's life as William

[10] Fiering 1981, p. 309

Ames, 'the spiritual father of the New England churches,' and Solomon Stoddard, his grandfather. Ames wrote, 'if the habit of vertue be absent though we should doe some good works, yet we are not rooted and grounded in good, but are rashly carried with evill and that goodness soone vanisheth.'[11] In similar vein, Stoddard wrote, 'moral virtues are acquired by practice, and accustoming themselves that way, will beget an habit. But grace is obtained by infusion.'[12] Both views represent a fairly common Reformed understanding of habit, that external habits cannot develop true virtue. Instead, true virtue must arise from a new, God-given, disposition which then gives rise to good works.

That Edwards's view of habit follows this pattern is clear from his own entries in his *Miscellanies*. In *Miscellanies* l, Edwards pointed out that true virtue cannot be acquired by habit. Instead there needs to be a real and decisive change in someone's life. He wrote,

> now it is certain that [in] every man that becomes good, there is a last moment of his being bad and a first moment of his being good, a last moment of his being in a state of damnation and a first moment of his being in a state of salvation; or thus, there is a time before which if he had died but one moment, he would have gone to hell, and after which if he had died but one moment, he would have gone to heaven: this is self-evident.[13]

In another entry from the following year, *Miscellanies* 73, he reiterated this view when he wrote, 'to say that a man who has no true virtue and no true grace can acquire it by frequent exercises of [it], is as much a contradiction as to say a man acts grace when he has no grace, or that he has it [when] he has it not.'[14] In these entries Edwards is stating an orthodox Reformed view.

It was a view that flew in the face of developments in his day that called Reformed and Puritan metaphysics into question. Edwards was resolutely opposed to the increasingly popular view espoused by John Locke, among others, who believed that mere custom or regularity was enough to inculcate truly virtuous habits. Edwards, in keeping with the Reformed tradition, did not regard habit as naked potential, but as the gift of God which would necessarily give rise to faith. Edwards would have concurred with the 'Reformed theologians [who] argued that after having received the habit of grace, one can never fall out of the state of grace, since the habit of faith as part of the new creature can never be lost.'[15]

The Significance of Practice in Edwards's Theology

Since habit is the necessary condition for true faith, which must then come to a realization, it becomes clear why practice is, for Edwards, such an important sign of true faith. As he stated, 'seeing that holy

[11] Cited in (Fiering, 1978, pp. 204–05)

[12] Cited in (Fiering, 1978, pp. 205)

Fig. 11: Alexander Comrie (1706–74)

[13] *WJE* 13:168–69
[14] *WJE* 13:242

[15] Wisse 2003, pp. 181–82

practice is the scope and aim of that which is the first ground of the bestowment of grace, it is doubtless the tendency of grace itself; otherwise it would follow that God makes use of a certain means to attain an end which is not fitted for that end, and has no tendency to it.'[16] The reason for Edwards's emphasis upon practice is to be found in the Reformed tradition that Edwards inherited where holiness of life was a necessary consequence of sanctifying grace in a person's life.

It was inconceivable for those in the Reformed tradition that someone who had been infused by the grace of God would not then go on to live a sanctified life. The believer who received the Spirit of God is infused with love for God. This love is manifested in a desire to obey God and to be conformed to the image of his Son. The work of the Holy Spirit pervades every aspect of the believer's life and affects every faculty. Although the Holy Spirit carries out distinctive works in the life of the saint, such as regeneration, justification, sanctification, etc., these works are inextricably linked and each implies the others. Universal holiness of life is the result of the necessary change that follows the real change that the Holy Spirit effects in the life of the Christian through the infusion of a new habit.

Where God has bestowed the habit of grace, its goal is holy practice. Consequently, practice was, for Edwards, a sure sign that the Holy Spirit is at work in a person's life. As Conrad Cherry notes, 'practice, the performance of good works, exhibits the nature of faith before the eyes of the man of faith as well as before God. Edwards claimed Christian practice as the chief means through which one may be assured that he is a man of faith.'[17] This theme of the importance of Christian practice is one that Edwards returned to repeatedly throughout his life.

From the 1720s onward, Edwards was particularly concerned with the idea of the evidences of true faith. As a result, he drew up several lists of the marks of true faith. Some of his more famous lists are found in *The Distinguishing Marks* and *The Religious Affections*. There were, however, lesser works listing signs of true spiritual experience such as *Directions for Judging of Persons' Experiences*.[18] In his notebook entitled Signs of Godliness, which dates from around 1728/9, Edwards took up the theme of the importance of practice in the Christian life.

He began the notebook with a number of biblical references to the importance of fruit bearing. This led him to conclude 'that this is a Scripture way of judging, to judge by fruits.'[19] This fruit, he went on to demonstrate from the Bible, included the fact that, 'following Christ's example as well as keeping his commandments, is a sign.'[20] This meant doing good works which are 'especially insisted on as evidential.'[21] Such practice was vital both in time and for eternity according to Edwards since 'God will judge men hereafter by the same things that he proves 'em by here.'[22] He then went on to outline in

[16] WJE 8:295

[17] Cherry 1990, p. 143

[18] WJE 21:522–24

[19] WJE 21:471

[20] WJE 21:472

[21] WJE 21:473

[22] WJE 21:475

detail the specific signs and practices, some thirty in total, which are the 'fruits of grace in the life.'[23]

The importance that Edwards placed upon Christian practice is also clear in his magnum opus on Christian experience, *The Religious Affections*. His twelfth and final distinguishing mark of holy affections is that 'gracious and holy affections have their exercise and fruit in Christian practice.'[24] It is not surprising that, of all the signs, this one should have received the greatest attention from Edwards since he concluded that

> Christian practice or a holy life is a great and distinguishing sign of true and saving grace. But I may go further, and assert, that it is the chief of all the signs of grace, both as an evidence of the sincerity of professors unto others, and also to their own conscience.[25]

One might dip into Edwards's writings at almost any point and find this same emphasis upon the importance of practice. So, for example, in 1739 in *Miscellanies* 790 he wrote,

> and by what the Scriptures have taught us in this matter, we must determine that good fruits, or good works and keeping Christ's commandments, are the evidences by which we are chiefly and most safely and surely to be determined, not only concerning the godliness of others, but also concerning our own godliness.[26]

Though holiness of life is perhaps the foremost theme in Edwards's work, there is in one sense little original that he has to say upon the subject. For, as John Gerstner wrote, 'in emphasizing sanctification Edwards was in the mainstream of the Puritan tradition.'[27] What is, if not distinctive, at least a particular emphasis in terms of Edwards's contribution is his recasting of the theme of holy living and practice less as a test whereby one might be assured of salvation, but as a means of identifying true faith in the aftermath of revival. It was a means which he believed would expose the shortcomings of many who had professed faith or exhibited some signs of spiritual life during the excitement of those days but had subsequently grown cold.

The Test of Practice

Perhaps Edwards's main contribution to the whole field of understanding religious experience is how this view of practice impacted his morphology of conversion. In many respects his views on conversion were both orthodox and conventional. In one important respect, however, his views were different from those of his New England predecessors and peers. Edwards's thought engineered a paradigm shift in how conversion was to be understood and evaluated. Previously in the New England tradition, conversion was authenticated in light of

[23] *WJE* 21:476

[24] *WJE* 2:383

[25] *WJE* 2:406

[26] *WJE* 18:474–76

[27] Gerstner 1991-93, 3:224

the Puritan understanding of preparation and the various steps that the preparation and conversion process followed. Edwards, while not completely rejecting the idea of preparation, turned this model upside down by setting aside the steps in the conversion process, to concentrate upon what was produced as a result of the conversion experience.

His rethinking of the model of authentic conversion came in part from his own conversion experience. As John Smith has written,

> Edwards obviously regarded his [conversion] experience as of monumental and life changing importance. Strangely enough, however, few historians have found this event worth describing or analysing, and even fewer have found this critical religious experience to bear any crucial consequences for his life and thought. Nevertheless, many features of Edwards' thought, in both form and content, can be traced directly to this signal existential moment when the whole of his religious identity and experience was shaped.[28]

Edwards's conversion experience shaped not only his thought in general, but also his thought about the conversion experience in particular. For his conversion was not the classic model of steps and degrees. Rather like Richard Baxter, in a previous generation, he came to discover that 'God breaketh not all men's hearts alike.'[29]

While his own conversion experience may have caused him to think again about the nature of true conversion, it was, as usual, the Bible itself which caused him to think most deeply about how true conversion may be identified. As he hinted in *Miscellanies* 317, if the current paradigm for conversion emphasizing certain steps before conversion was insisted upon then, it was at variance with the conversions that were found in the Bible.[30] In a sermon in 1752 he noted that, 'too much stress has been laid by many persons, on a great work of the law, preceding their comforts.'[31] He also noted the serious outcome of this was that by insisting upon this model of preparationism 'very many have been deceived, and established in a false hope.'[32]

For Edwards, the nub of the matter was that insistence upon the preparationist model opened the door for Satan to deceive people by imitating the conversion process. Yet, while Satan might emulate the process, the one thing he could not reproduce was the fruit of true faith. Writing in the 1734 sermon, 'False Light and True,' he described Satan as 'God's ape' and noted, 'there are counterfeit graces and a counterfeit light that the devil oftentimes flatters men in and influences them to depend upon, instead of true grace and the true saving light of God's spirit. Every grace has its counterfeit.'[33]

The importance of practice in the Christian life, and how this relates to Edwards's concept of habit becomes clear in *Charity and Its Fruits*, Sermon 10, where he examined Paul's words '[love] rejoiceth not in iniquity, but rejoiceth in the truth.' Edwards viewed this text as a

[28] Smith 1992, p. 52

[29] Murray 1980, p. 19

[30] WJE 13:397–400

[31] WJE 25:622

[32] WJE 25:622

[33] WJE 19:127

summary verse of 'all other good tendencies of charity.'[34] From it, he established the doctrine, 'all true grace tends to holy practice.' He saw that iniquity is here equated with wicked 'deeds or practice'[35] and truth with 'holy practice or well-doing.'[36] He wrote,

> this seems to be the design of the Apostle here, to show that charity is opposite to all unrighteousness, or evil doings or practice, and that it tends to all holy practice. And charity being here spoken of by the Apostle as the sum of all true and sincere grace, the doctrine which has been observed, viz. that all true grace tends to holy practice, is fully contained in the words [of the text].[37]

He added that the reason that this is the case is because grace 'infused' into the heart is an active principle. Edwards then continued to develop the sermon by first of all pointing to the arguments which supported the idea that all true Christian grace tends towards holy practice. In doing so, he outlined five arguments. The first argument is that Christian practice is the scope and the end of election. The second is that Christ by his death 'has purchased grace and holiness for the elect.'[38] This is the 'end' of his work of redemption. Thirdly, it is for the purpose of holy practice that God infuses grace into the life of the believer. Fourthly, he argued that 'a true knowledge of God and divine things is a practical knowledge.'[39] It is not merely a speculative knowledge. It is the absence of such knowledge that leads wicked men to practice iniquity.

While these arguments are rooted in Scripture, Edwards's fifth argument has to do with the nature of the principle of grace itself. It is this argument that he develops most fully. His investigation of the nature of the principle of grace is again divided into five points. The first is that grace tends towards practice because it is seated immediately in the will. It is from the will that all men's practices are directed. His second point is that grace is, by its very definition, a principle of action because it is a principle of holiness. Like all principles, this principle tends towards action. He wrote, 'it is absurd to talk of a principle that does not tend to practice.'[40] Thirdly, he wrote that that which is real, as opposed to that which is a mere shadow, is effectual. Fourthly, he pointed out that the principle of grace is, according to Scripture, a principle of life. It must therefore overflow into activity. His fifth, and final point, is that Scripture underlines the fact that we must recognize that grace is 'an exceedingly powerful principle'[41] and the more powerful a principle is, the more it will tend towards practice.

There is in Edwards's argument the idea that grace works in accordance with a principle like any other principle. However, it is important to note how Edwards's argument concerning the tendency of grace towards practice develops. Significantly, his first four arguments are all scriptural arguments, each one offering at least one biblical text in

[34] *WJE* 8:293

[35] *WJE* 8:294
[36] *WJE* 8:294

[37] *WJE* 8:294

[38] *WJE* 8:295

[39] *WJE* 8:296

[40] *WJE* 8:298

[41] *WJE* 8:299

support. Edwards's convictions regarding practice are first and foremost biblical convictions. It is only once he has established the biblical foundations for his case, that he then turns to a more general consideration of the principle of grace itself and how it operates as a principle. In this argument concerning the nature of grace we find elements of psychology, e.g., the relationship of the will to the understanding; of the overall nature of principle—that it has a tendency toward actions; and of explicit biblical argument. Typically, Edwards wants to demonstrate that his case is biblical and that since it is biblical it is also demonstrable by reason.

As Edwards then went on to outline twelve ways in which grace has a tendency towards practice, he again combined the biblical and the rational. In each case, it is Edwards's contention that it is practice that demonstrates the reality of the work of grace in the life of the individual.

Reading through Edwards's corpus, it is clear that he emphasised the fact that the principle infused by God in regeneration was reflected in practice. So he wrote in his sermon 'Profitable Hearers of the Word', in which he frequently referred to 1 Corinthians, that 'there is a principle of spiritual life infused into the soul in conversion that exerts itself in holy acts and exercises.'[42] Furthermore, he stated in 'A Divine and Supernatural Light' that,

> in the renewing and sanctifying work of the Holy Ghost, those things are wrought in the soul that are above nature, and of which there is nothing of the like kind in the soul by nature; and they are caused to exist in the soul habitually, and according to such a stated constitution or law, that lays such a foundation for exercises in a continual course, as is called a principle of nature.[43]

Yet care must be taken not to press this language of habit, law and principle too far. There is nothing mechanical about it. For Edwards recognized that there is considerable variety in the work of the Holy Spirit in the life of the individual.

This is seen, for example, in a 1740 sermon on Luke 22:32, that 'those that have true grace in their hearts may yet stand in great need of being converted.'[44] In the course of the sermon he pointed out how terms such as conversion, new creation, putting off the old and putting on the new, opening the eyes of the blind and raising the dead are used in the New Testament not only to describe God's first work of grace, but his ongoing work in the life of the believer. As such, the life of a believer is one of ongoing conversion by 'God's Spirit carrying grace to higher degrees in their souls.'[45] In other words, he saw sanctification as a progressive work where sometimes, when grace is first infused, it is but as a small dawning of light, like the first beginnings of the light in the dawning of the day; and the first actings of faith are feeble, appearing

[42] WJE 14:258

[43] WJE 17:411

[44] WJE 22:184

[45] WJE 22:186

chiefly in holy desires after Christ and holiness, but not attended with clear satisfaction.[46]

So the whole of the saint's life is a work of complete renovation by God. He then added that, 'in every step and degree of that restoration, something is brought out of nothing, and there is the same almighty creating power needed and exerted in every step of the work, as at the beginning of this work in first conversion.'[47] The principle is there, but just as there is no formula that brings about conversion, so there is no formula for the ongoing work of Holy Spirit in the individual's life. Rather, the Spirit operates according to his own sovereign will and purpose in the life of the saint. Sometimes he operates more forcefully than at other times. Also, the believer can 'improve' upon him by attending to the means of grace or he might quench his influence by neglect.

So, while Edwards spoke in terms of a principle or habit at work in the life of believers, great care must be taken in considering what he does or does not mean by that. The operation of this principle is not an unbridled force, nor does it abrogate human responsibility. This is evident when we glimpse his view of the struggle for sanctification.

Practice and The Struggle for Sanctification

Despite the fact that Edwards pressed the test of practice because he wished to warn hypocrites, it is also evident from his writings that he was not a perfectionist. Edwards was well aware of the indwelling power of sin in the human heart.

Speaking in 1731 of self-examination before the Lord's Supper, he stated that it is 'not every unfitness that renders the attendance defective and sinful … A man having so much sin in his heart that he can do no other than attend the Lord's Supper in a very defective manner is not the unfitness we speak of.'[48] Likewise, he noted in a sermon of 1737, that while saints should strive for perfection, 'godly men never do actually attain to perfect holiness in this life, but are always very far from it. The most holy men have found cause to complain of the abundance of the corruption that they found remaining in their hearts.'[49] Indeed, in *Some Thoughts Concerning the Revival* he cautioned against those who were too swift to examine the religious experience of others and to conclude that they were hypocrites.[50]

Edwards saw the whole work of God from conversion to glorification as one of 'renovation.'[51] In this renovation man is restored to his pristine state. The work of conversion is a work of creation 'and the new creature is not fully made till all that creature is remade which is destroyed by the fall, which was the destruction of the old creation.'[52] As a result of this, Edwards concluded that, 'grace is very imperfect in

[46] *WJE* 22:186

[47] *WJE* 22:190

[48] *WJE* 17:267

[49] *WJE* 19:684

[50] *WJE* 4:474

[51] *WJE* 4:190

[52] *WJE* 4:190

all, and all stand not only in need of some addition of grace to mend small defects, but they all stand in need of a great change, very much altering them from their present state.'[53]

While Edwards was confident that the infusion of the habit of grace into a person's life would have an unfailing outcome, he was nonetheless realistic about regenerated human nature and its ongoing struggle with the old sinful nature. In *Religious Affections* he wrote, 'such is the nature of grace, and of true spiritual light, that they naturally dispose the saints in the present state, to look upon their grace and godliness little, and their deformity great.'[54] In respect of this he quoted Luther, 'this remains to him that has begun to be a Christian, to think that he is not yet a Christian, but to seek that he may be a Christian, that he may glory with Paul, 'I am not but I desire to be'; a Christian not yet finished, but only in his beginnings.'[55]

[53] *WJE* 4:194

[54] *WJE* 2:323

[55] *WJE* 2:323

Jonathan Edwards and Ratiocination: An Eternal Journey into the Discovery of God and Truth

TOBY K. EASLEY

As Jonathan Edwards pondered understanding and sensing God, he undoubtedly contemplated the present limitations of human knowledge and the senses, in comparison to a future expanding knowledge and sense of an infinite God. The word "ratiocination" is associated with the Latin term *ratiocinari,* and philosophers such as John Locke used it to refer to human reason. Edwards more than likely interacted with the term in his mind when reading Locke and others. Nevertheless, Edwards, using his own theological and philosophical prism, expanded on the word in order to contemplate the eternal implications of knowing God now and in eternity. Ratiocination can also be defined as the process of "exact thinking," "a reasoned train of thought," or "the process of logical reasoning." As Edwards realized the limitations of man's understanding and reason, he contemplated within his notebook "The Mind," that "ratiocination" for those lacking "perfect ideas of all things at once"—for instance, all humanity—is the process of "finding out truth."[1]

For the purpose of exploring an overview of Edwards's thoughts on ratiocination, four particular vantage points will be discussed. First, spiritual light is a necessity for discovering sound spiritual truth in the process of ratiocination. Second, a type of ratiocination occurs in other disciplines such as science and philosophy, but does not assume these truths discovered are always accompanied by spiritual light. Third, a distinction exists between ratiocination in the mind and human sensory discoveries. Fourth, ratiocination in this world is only a type of the fuller knowledge to be attained throughout eternity for the Christian, and will transition into discovering God's infinite truths and "beauty and excellence"[2] for all eternity.

Naturally, as one scrutinizes Edwards, to say he used the term "rati-

[1] *WJE* 6:342. Edwards wrote, "Therefore, if we had perfect ideas of all things at once, that is, could have all in one view, we should know all truth at the same moment, and there would be no such thing as ratiocination or finding out truth."

[2] *WJE* 6:332–36. Edwards defined these terms "excellency" and "beauty" as "Excellency therefore seems to consist in equality. Thus, if there be two perfect equal circles or globes together, there is something more of beauty than if they were of unequal, disproportionate magnitudes. And if two parallel lines be drawn, the beauty is greater than if they were obliquely inclined without proportion, because there is equality of distance. And if, betwixt two parallel lines, two equal circles be placed, each at the same distance from each parallel line ... the beauty is greater than if they stood at irregular distances from the parallel lines" (332–33). Additionally, he broke down "beauty" into two categories: "simple" and "complex." In using the example of perpendicular lines not in perfect proportion, he wrote they could still qualify as "simple beauty." However, "Proportion is complex beauty ... Thus, when the distance between two is exactly equal, their distance is their relation one to another; the distance is the same, the bodies are two, wherefore this is their correspondency and beauty" (333–34). He further

expanded his thoughts on "excellency" by claiming, "Excellency consists in the similarness of one being to another—not merely equality and proportion, but any kind of similarness . . . One of the highest excellencies is love, As nothing else has a proper being but spirits, and as bodies are but the shadow of being, therefore, the consent of bodies to one another, and the harmony that is among them, is but the shadow of excellency, The highest excellency, therefore, must be the consent of spirits one to another" (336–37).

[3] WJE 17:57

[4] WJE 2:244. Edwards used several Old Testament examples and wrote, "And we have manifest instances of it in Scripture; as in the children of Israel, who sang God's praises at the Red Sea, but soon forgat God's works."

[5] WJE 6:342

[6] WJE 17:63

[7] WJE 17:63

[8] WJE 17:63

[9] WJE 6:342

ocination" exclusively with only one of these definitions would be to deny the complex theological, philosophical, and practical methods that his mind often exemplified. In his sermon "The Pure in Heart Blessed," he threads together human reason and experience and, according to Mark Valeri, Edwards "clearly adumbrates" his sermon, "A Divine and Supernatural Light."[3] In some of these earlier works, overtones of some of his later works are present, such as *Religious Affections*. For instance, he speaks of those who witnessed God performing great miracles in the Old Testament, but they persisted without a true sense of knowing the Lord salvifically in their hearts.[4] This thought concept spread into many facets of Edwards's ministry for the remainder of his life. His sermon, "The Pure in Heart Blessed" preceded the 1734-1735 Revival, the 1740s "Great Awakening," and his 1750 dismissal from Northampton. However, in all of these life-altering revivals and the tendentious ending of his ministry in Northampton, Edwards remained steadfast in believing an increasing knowledge and sense of God impacted both the mind and actions of Christians. Additionally, Edwards expressed in "The Mind," regarding God and truth, "Hence we see in how strict a sense it may be said, that God is truth itself."[5] Furthermore, ratiocination expanded beyond this world in a more perfect sense and would eventually lead to greater things for His children in eternity, because God would continually reveal the magnitude of His infinite knowledge and infinite nature.

With God as "truth itself," Edwards believed all humanity depended on spiritual light from God as a necessity for discovering sound truth through our finite ratiocination. Consequently, from his writings in "The Mind," beginning in 1723, until preaching "The Pure in Heart Blessed" in 1730, he established his own definition of terms. First, to speak of the "eyes" is to understand the concept of seeing things with "the eyes of the body," and the concept of seeing "with the eye of the soul."[6] According to Edwards, the latter of the two is "vastly nobler" than the former. In order to see things with the soul, our "intellectual powers" should not be "neglected and disused."[7] In other words, when we see things with our physical eyes, human passions kick in, and a war takes place with reason and passion. When we view through the "eye of the soul,"[8] God gives spiritual strength along with reason for the situation. Extraordinary moments such as these, however, are temporary in this life for the Christian, because the flesh will continue to struggle against the soul. The way for the Christian to garner hope in all of the world's pitfalls is to look beyond our limited ratiocination in this life and envision the perfect state in heaven. In "The Mind," Edwards states some perceptions about mankind's finite limitations. "Reasoning is only of use to us in consequence of the paucity of our ideas, and because we can have but very few in view at once."[9] Due to these human deficiencies in the here-and-now, "A true sense of the glory of [God] is that which never can be got by ratiocination."[10] Theologically, he joyfully proclaimed, "It is evident that all things are self-evident to God."[11] Finite human beings on the other hand need spiritual illumination for enhanced ratiocination regarding biblical truth in the present, as well as the perfecting of it in perpetuity.

Edwards pointed out that a type of ratiocination occurs in relation to other academic disciplines, but this does not assume truths discovered are always accompanied with spiritual light. In other words, "light" is not always accompanied with "heat" in both the heart and the mind.[12] Therefore, ratiocination takes on a new extraordinary dimension for the Christian. At certain times and in various ways, through spiritual light and the eyes of faith, a Christian may have wisdom to discern scientific and philosophical error and potential false teachings in light of God's Word. Edwards commented regarding Paul's preaching in Athens, "Upon this Paul rises up in the midst of 'em and makes a speech to 'em. And, as he speaks to philosophers and men of learning, in how different a manner [he] speaks to 'em: there is evidently a greater depth in his discourse, and philosophical ratiocination, and height of style than in his ordinary discourse to common men, such as would be likely to draw the attention and gain the assent of philosophers."[13] Edwards made the distinction between Paul's philosophical knowledge and where the trail of human philosophy ends. In other words, the Greek philosophers taught at a high level while mixing in truth, but they ultimately concluded ἐν σοφίᾳ ἀνθρώπων, "In the wisdom of men." However, prior to and ever since Paul's Damascus Road experience, Edwards discovered that all believers, along with Paul, share a kindred spirit of subjective experience, ἐν δυνάμει θεοῦ, "In the power of God" (1 Corinthians 2:5). Ultimately, this advantage of godly wisdom enhanced the believers' discernment and abilities in ratiocination through spiritual light. In reality, the philosophers of Athens, and many other intellectuals of the world would never rise beyond their state of spiritual deadness and blindness while remaining outside of Christ. Under the topic of "Spiritual Knowledge," in his *Miscellanies*, Edwards concluded, "Ratiocination, without this spiritual light, never will give one such an advantage to see things in their true relations and respects to other things and to things in general."[14]

Edwards also never denied that a general type of Ratiocination exists with all humanity. However, true "sight" through illumined ratiocination can only be attained by "conversion," and, by this, Edwards claimed, "They are brought to see spiritual objects."[15] In fact, he said, "They now see the truth of spiritual things which before they were uncertain about."[16] Consequently, although possessing a knowledge of God and of Christ and His glory is certainly commendable, he clarified,

[10] *WJE* 17:64

[11] *WJE* 17:64

[12] *WJE* 2:31. Smith accurately wrote, "In the Affections no less than in other writings he refused to oppose the religious conception of spirit to intellectual pursuits, and he did not join forces with popular revivalism, which sets understanding over against the 'having of the spirit.' 'Holy affections,' Edwards always held, 'are not heat without light; but evermore arise from some information of the understanding, some spiritual instruction that the mind receives, some light or actual knowledge.' On the other hand, there are many affections entirely unrelated to such understanding, and of them he says, 'it is a sure evidence that these affections are not spiritual, let them be ever so high.'"

[13] *WJE* 14:510

[14] *WJE* 13:470. The words preceding this quote from "Miscellanies" no. 408 are very important. Edwards began by explaining, "When the ideas themselves appear more lively, and with greater strength and impression, as the ideas of spiritual things do [to] one that is spiritually enlightened, their circumstances and various relations and connections between themselves and with other ideas appear more; there are more of these habitudes and respects taken notice of, and they also are more clearly discerned: and therefore hereby a man sees the harmony between spiritual things, and so [comes] to be convinced of their truth." In the ensuing paragraph following the quote from no. 408, associated with fn 14, Edwards continued, "A man that sets himself to reason without divine light is like a man that goes in the dark into a garden full of the most beautiful plants, and most artfully ordered, and compares things together by going from one thing to another, to feel of them and to measure the distances; but he that sees by divine light is like a man that views the garden when the sun shines upon it."

[15] *WJE* 17:322

[16] *WJE* 17:322

[17] *WJE* 17:322

[18] Sermon no. 156, *WJEO* 45

[19] *WJE* 17:322–23

[20] *WJE* 17:323

[21] *WJE* 17:422

[22] *WJE* 17:54

[23] *WJE* 17:54

[24] *WJE* 17:422

[25] *WJE* 17:422

[26] *WJE* 2:206, 2074–75. On this subject Edwards specifically said, "Hence the work of the Spirit of God in regeneration is often in Scripture compared to the giving a new sense, giving eyes to see, and ears to hear, unstopping the ears of the deaf, and opening the eyes of them that were born blind, and turning from darkness unto light" (2:206). Furthermore, Edwards later elaborated, "Well therefore may the Scripture represent those who are destitute of that spiritual sense, by which is perceived the beauty of holiness, as totally blind, deaf and senseless, yea dead. And well may regeneration, in which this divine sense is given to the soul by its Creator, be represented as opening the blind eyes, and raising the dead, and bringing a person into a new world. For if what has been said be considered, it will be manifest, that when a person has this sense and knowledge given him, he will view nothing as he did before; though before he knew all things after the flesh, yet henceforth he will know them so no more; and he is become 'a new creature, old things are passed away, behold all things are become new'; agreeable to II Cor. 5:16–17" (2:274–75).

" 'Tis not merely by ratiocination that those things are confirmed to them."[17] In a sermon on Romans 4:16, Edwards proclaimed, "Thus the disciples they believed and were sure that their master was 'the Christ, the son of the living God' (John 6:69). Not that they were convinced by ratiocination merely, for flesh and blood had not revealed it to 'em as Christ tells Peter (Matthew 16:17). But the Father in heaven had revealed it to 'em, the divine Glory of their master."[18]

To explain himself further regarding authentic sight of spiritual truth and understanding, he used an astronomical and agrarian example. "A man that looks on visible objects, on the sun or earth and fields, is not convinced by ratiocination of their being, but by sight; the light that shines shows these things to be. So there is a spiritual light that shines into men's hearts that shows spiritual objects to have a being."[19] Here and in other places, Edwards alludes to the sun and its light and even emphasizes the light of the sun as a type of the light of Jesus Christ.

As he expanded his thoughts on spiritual light and how it causes the Christian to discern the Divine in the "visible" creation, he said that with new eyes it caused one to view the "sun, moon, and stars" as brightly shining "with a new kind of light, even spiritual light."[20] He explained these two steps further by saying, "seeing the truth of religion from hence, is by reason; though it be but by one step."[21] This is precisely why in his sermon entitled "Practical Atheism," Edwards described the hearts of atheists and wicked men as naturally floundering in "stupidity, folly, and sottishness."[22] These individuals not only ignore the obvious "evidences of his being," they push aside "obvious" and "discoverable by reason, by a long train of ratiocination."[23] However, Edwards is in no way perplexed by their "folly," because he explained that understanding the "beauty" of God and his creation is preceded by "divine light" and "reason has to do in that accepting of, and trusting in Christ, that is consequent on it."[24] Therefore, all individuals both righteous and wicked have an ability to reason, but the Christian integrates both Divine light and ratiocination through the Word of God in their filtering of theology, science, philosophy, astronomy, agriculture and so forth. Although ratiocination and the ability through Divine light to see God's "beauty" are to Edwards separate parts of the whole, he did not fail to explain himself. "Reason's work is to perceive truth, and not excellency."[25] However, to grow truly in understanding Divine "beauty" and "excellency," illumined ratiocination had to play an important role. Edwards's complex system was a both/and solution, not either/or. Furthermore, Divine "light," which Edwards also associated with regeneration, needed to take precedence over cultured ratiocination, in order for the light to illuminate any potential darkness of human discovery.[26]

Other important distinctions for Edwards were the differentiations between ratiocination simply in the mind and human sensory discoveries. Differentiating between the recognition of objective truth and subjectively experiencing the impact in the heart is what Edwards resonated in his sermon "The Pure in Heart Blessed."[27] As he preached he warned his congregation, "The wicked spirits in the other world, they doubtless [have] more immediate apprehensions of the being of God, and his power and wrath, than the wicked have in this world."[28] He wanted to be clear that even if you are "told what sort of being he is and what he has done and are told right," he went on to conclude, "this is not that beatific, happifying sight of God."[29] Consequently, by having an objective scriptural knowledge of God and "his being almighty and all-wise and good, by ratiocination, that is not what the Scripture calls seeing God."[30] Edwards describes a real sensory experience as an "immediate discovery, that must give the mind a real sense of the excellency and beauty of God." He elaborates, "The discoveries that the saints have of God's excellency and grace here, they are immediate in a sense; that is, they don't depend on ratiocination."[31] Here, Edwards is not nullifying "ratiocination;" rather, he is stressing the distinction between the Christian's subjective spiritual experiences and ratiocination. For Edwards, the unfortunate attribute of these "immediate discoveries" in this world, both during and following our conversion, is the temporary nature of these epiphanal moments when we sense God's "beauty." However, a glorious hope is coming, because the "temptations" and "doubtings" that occur here *pro tem* will be excluded, because Edwards assured his congregation these interruptions of glorious experiences will not occur in heaven.[32]

Over three years later, Edwards would drive his objective and subjective analysis home again in his sermon, "A Divine and Supernatural Light."[33] He looked into many of the same eyes and faces of his congregation and said, " 'Tis not ratiocination that gives men the perception of the beauty and amiableness of countenance; though it may be many ways indirectly an advantage to it, ... Reason may determine that a countenance is beautiful to others; it may determine that honey is sweet to others; but it will never give me a perception of its sweetness."[34] In other words, the beauty of God's Word is one thing, but for the individual to have the Spirit of God allow him or her to sense truly that beauty in a pure form objectively and subjectively, was a heavenly experience on earth.[35] The same stood true in comparison to seeing honey, and then actually tasting the honey. The wicked through ratiocination were capable of human reasoning regarding God, whether they believed or denied His existence. However, according to the Northampton Sage, ratiocination and knowledge minus Divine light equaled spiritual blindness and a continual absence of a spiritual sense. In Edwards's own way of putting it, a lost man or woman could see honey, but they would

[27] *WJE* 17:57–86

[28] *WJE* 17:64

[29] *WJE* 17:63

[30] *WJE* 17:63

[31] *WJE* 17:65

[32] *WJE* 17:65

[33] *WJE* 17:408–26

[34] *WJE* 17:422–23

[35] *WJE* 17:423–25. In this section of "A Divine and Supernatural Light," Edwards gives extensive elaboration to what occurs when one experiences the "light" subjectively along with the illumination of God's Word objectively. With conviction he told his audience, "Yea, the least glimpse of the glory of God in the face of Christ doth more exalt and ennoble the

soul, than all the knowledge of those that have the greatest speculative understanding in divinity, without grace. This knowledge has the most noble object that is, or can be, viz. the divine glory, and excellency of God, and Christ ... This knowledge is that which is above all others sweet and joyful. Men have a great deal of pleasure in human knowledge, in studies of natural things; but this is nothing to that joy which arises from this divine light shining into the soul ... This knowledge will wean from the world, and raise the inclination to heavenly things ... And it convinces of the reality of those glorious rewards that God has promised to them that obey him."

[36] WJE 17:423

[37] WJE 8:469–74

[38] WJE 8:443

[39] WJE 8:459

[40] WJE 8:459

[41] WJE 8:531

never truly taste the honey of spiritual things in an unregenerate state, because perceiving "the sweetness of honey; always depended on the enlightened sense of the heart."[36]

As he gazed into the eschaton and viewed the everlasting progress of ratiocination, Edwards believed the ability of the Christian to find truth in this world is only a type of the fuller knowledge to be attained throughout eternity and that God's people will progressively discover God's infinite truths in His presence for all eternity. The characteristic pattern with Edwards on most theological topics was to exhaust it as far as Scripture would allow. Where does "finding out truth" and "ratiocination" ultimately end up for Edwards? For him, a fuller and more complete knowledge was to be attained throughout eternity that will continually satisfy our desire to know God more and to experience the "beauty" of His Divine being. If God is infinite, how long will "ratiocination" or "finding out truth" occur? What will our experience be like in the presence of God's "beauty" and "excellence" for all eternity? Quite normal for Edwards's deep thinking was to consider a subject to the nth degree.

To find Edwards's answer to the above question, one must ponder his definition of the chief end, in his "Dissertation Concerning the End."[37] One concept he introduced was God's desire to make Himself known to His redeemed people throughout all eternity. Furthermore, God's desire to be one with His people is why He will bring them home and unite them to Himself. He believed this was a direct fulfillment of Jesus' words: "that they all may be one, as thou Father art in me, and I in thee, that they also may be one in us; I in them and thou in me, that they may be made perfect in one" (John 17:21, 23).[38] God's purpose then in communicating His fullness is for Himself, because their good He desires "is so much in union and communion with himself."[39] The infinite nature of His people's good then goes back to when God made the world, because even then God viewed the entire duration and its eternal progression and union and communion with Himself, because "the nearer anything comes to infinite, the nearer it comes to an identity with God."[40] This is God's way of communicating His divine fullness as "the fountain" of living streams and as the "beams of the sun are something of the sun ... The beams of glory come from God, are something of God, and are refunded back again to their original. So that the whole is of God, and in God, and to God: and he is the beginning, and the middle, and the end."[41]

How far would Edwards actually go in his explanation of John 17:21, 23? He was willing to admit humbly that it was impossible for him to express in totality the infinite purpose of God in bringing His people into oneness. However, he did go so far as to express his faith in God's infinite promises as far as his finite mind could express from

Scripture. "I suppose it will not be denied by any, that God, in glorifying the saints in heaven with eternal felicity, aims to satisfy his infinite grace or benevolence, by the bestowment of a good infinitely valuable, because eternal: and yet there never will come the moment, when it can be said, that now this infinitely valuable good has been actually bestowed."[42] Therefore, ratiocination in "finding out truth" and sensing Divine "beauty" and "excellence" exists eternally for the Christian in both the objective and subjective realms. In eternity, however, both our increasing knowledge of God and our uninterrupted sense of unity with God will extend in perpetuity. Oliver Crisp accurately analyzed Edwards's thought process on the subject by claiming, "The idea Edwards has is that the creature is in a relationship to God that will become ever more intimate, but which will never issue in the creature becoming identical to the creator."[43] Therefore, although this is an eternal theosis of sorts, ratiocination or "finding out truth," and experiencing the "beauty" of the Divine for God's redeemed people, will both continue in infinity, in an infinite perfect state, according to Edwards, for "THE GLORY OF GOD."[44]

[42] *WJE* 8:536

[43] Crisp 2012, p. 83

[44] *WJE* 8:526. Capitalization was used for emphasis in Edwards's text.

Jonathan Edwards: America's Theologian? A Latino Evaluation of Jonathan Edwards's Harmartiology

CHRIS WOZNICKI

Introduction

It has been said that Jonathan Edwards is "America's theologian." Many would agree with this claim, and the theologian that has best articulated this claim is Robert Jenson in his book *America's Theologian: A Recommendation of Jonathan Edwards.* There are various reasons why Jenson believes that Edwards is "America's theologian." For instance, one reason that Jenson believes that Edwards is America's theologian is that Edwards's "achievement in the discipline of theology is the most weighty to have appeared on this continent."[1] However, Jenson's primary reason for believing that Edwards is America's theologian is because Edwards meets the problems and opportunities of American Christianity and the nation molded by it.[2] Jenson argues, "America and its church are the nation and church that the Enlightenment made."[3] As he expounds upon this claim, it is clear that he sees the Enlightenment as the defining narrative of Christianity in America. Edwards was a theologian who knew what to make of the enlightenment, "he was at once believing and enlightening."[4] Thus he is in a position to speak to the American Christianity that the Enlightenment created.

What Jenson argues for is both important and insightful. However, we must ask several important questions regarding Jenson's understanding of Edwards as "America's theologian." Which America is Jenson talking about? What is the defining narrative of American Christianity? Is the defining narrative the Enlightenment or is it something else? Are there other narratives that also explain and give meaning to American Christianity? Do the narratives of Asian Americans count as important American narratives? Should the narrative of African-Americans, from the "importing" of their ancestors to the civil rights

[1] Jenson 1988, p. 3

[2] Jenson 1988, p. 3
[3] Jenson 1988, p. 3

[4] Jenson 1988, p. 3

movement, be considered one of the defining American stories as well? What about the narrative of Latinos? The Latino Christian narrative is older than the Anglo-American Christian narrative. Latinos have been practicing their faith, predominately in a Roman Catholic form, among the Native Americans since before Anglo-American colonists arrived to this continent. We must also consider that there is a "Latino Evangelical" narrative. The Latino Evangelical population is growing rapidly. For instance, the April 15, 2013 issue of *Time* magazine featured a cover story titled "The Latino Reformation: Inside the New Hispanic Churches Transforming Religion in America." This article documents the fact that Latino Catholics, especially younger ones, are moving towards evangelical churches. The article also cites research done by the Pew Research Center stating that there are 2,500 Latino Assemblies of God churches, 3,200 Latino Southern Baptist churches, and 40,800 member churches in the National Hispanic Leadership Conference. All this to say, Latino Evangelicals are numerous and their population is growing fast. With this rapid growth, the Latino perspective will become increasingly important within Evangelical theological discussion. If we do in fact consider this particular narrative as an important part of the American story, and Edwards is truly to be regarded as America's theologian, he must be able to speak into this story as well.

In this paper I will examine the claim that Edwards is "America's theologian" by evaluating one particular piece of his theology, his *hamartiology*, in light of a Latino context. If Edwards's theology can be read productively from a Latino context, then we have good reason to say that he is "America's theologian."[5]

We will begin to evaluate Edwards as "America's theologian" by examining his answer to the question: Why do humans need to be redeemed? Having done this, I will present one critical criterion for evaluating Edwards's theology from a Latino perspective. This criterion is "community," specifically as it is presented in Justo Gonzalez's theology. By examining the theology of Edwards and Gonzalez, it will become apparent that Edwards's theology and Latino theology have a communal rather than individualistic understanding of responsibility and action. Thus, in this particular area Edwards can speak constructively to Latino theology and we can say that there are some grounds for calling him "America's Theologian."

Edwards's Soteriology

Why Humans Need Redemption

As a theologian in the Reformed tradition, Edwards places an emphasis on original sin. However, his articulation of the doctrine deviates

[5] This task can and should be performed from a variety of contexts, for instance we might want to see if Edwards can be productively read from an African-American context or an Asian-American context.

slightly from the typical Calvinistic view of this doctrine. This goes to show that even within one tradition, definitions of this doctrine vary. However, one definition which seems uncontroversial is the definition put forth by Oliver Crisp, in which he says that this doctrine is "the idea that Adam passed on to his progeny some terrible vitiation of moral nature due to the fall, resulting in its propagation to his posterity."[6] Although most Reformed theologians would agree with this broad definition, disagreement often arises as to the means by which original sin is imputed to Adam's descendants. Crisp explains that within the tradition there are two major understandings of the means by which original sin is imputed. The first is that it is imputed immediately, that is "in virtue of some metaphysical unity that is established between Adam and his posterity," the second is that it is imputed mediately, that "through some hereditary corruption which is passed down the generations from Adam onwards."[7] Having defined these terms: original sin, immediate imputation, and mediate imputation, we are now in a position to analyze Edward's answer to the question "Why do humans need redemption?"

The straightforward answer to the question at hand is that humans need redemption because they are sinners. A more nuanced answer to the question would seek to explain why all of humanity is guilty of sin, thus explaining why humanity needs redemption. In Edwards's defense of the doctrine of original sin, he tries to explain why it is that all humans are guilty of sin. In Edward's day, the doctrine was coming under attack from various English "Arminians," like John Taylor. One key objection put forth by these "Arminians" is that imputing Adam's guilt to his descendants is "unjust and unreasonable inasmuch as Adam and his posterity are not one and the same."[8] In other words, you can't blame Adam's children for what Adam did. Because Edwards is committed to the doctrine of original sin, he attempts to provide an answer as to why humans can indeed be blamed for the sin of Adam.

The Reformed tradition has traditionally given two explanations as to how original sin is imputed immediately: the Augustinian realist interpretation and the Federalist interpretation. The Augustinian realist school sees Adam as a concrete universal of humankind, thus humanity is dealt with "in him."[9] In this view Adam's descendants are somehow present in Adam when Adam committed the original sin. Thus all humanity actually sinned in Adam since all humanity actually shares in Adam's being. Another way of understanding the Augustinian realist position is that all humanity actually shares in Adam's human nature thus all humanity actually sinned in Adam.[10] The other view that has been popular in the Reformed tradition is the Federalist interpretation of original sin. Under this view, Adam is not seen as being in union with humanity, as the Augustinian view does, rather Adam is a repre-

[6] Crisp 2010, p. 50

[7] Crisp 2010, p. 51

[8] Crisp 2010, p. 66

[9] Crisp 2010, p. 51

[10] Crisp 2010, p. 51

11 WJE 3:107

12 WJE 3:107

13 WJE 18:348

14 WJE 18:348

15 Crisp 2010, p. 59
16 Hodge 1960, 2:208
17 McClymond and McDermott 2012, p. 351

18 Crisp 2010, p. 67

sentative of his race. These are the two views that Edwards is working with in formulating his doctrine of original sin. Let us now turn to Edwards's own account of original sin.

Edwards distinguishes between two ways that the phrase "original sin" is used. First, it is used to speak of the "innate sinful depravity of the heart."[11] In addition to this use, Edwards says that more commonly the phrase is used to refer to "the imputation of Adam's first sin; or in other words, the liableness of exposedness of Adam's posterity in divine judgment, to partake of the punishment of that sin."[12] It is this latter use of the phrase "original sin" with which we are concerned.

Although Edwards's longest and most well know treatment of this doctrine is found in his posthumously published book *Original Sin*, there are certain entries in his *Miscellanies* which shed light upon his beliefs regarding this doctrine. One such entry is *Miscellanies* entry number 717. In drawing from Thomas Ridgley's *Body of Divinity*, Edwards explains that Adam was the "federal head of his posterity, though he was their natural head, or common father."[13] As soon as Adam sinned he broke the covenant of works, resulting in terrible consequences which were "devolved upon us," the rest of humanity.[14] That is, none of the blessings contained within that covenant could be conveyed to us through our federal head and common father Adam. This particular entry displays the tension between a Federalist and an Augustinian understanding of this doctrine; Edwards uses both Federalist language ("federal head of his posterity") and Augustinian realist language ("natural head or common father") in this passage.

How shall we interpret Edwards's doctrine of original sin in light of this passage? Most interpreters have seen Edwards as standing somehow within the Federalist tradition. For instance, B.B. Warfield argues that Edwards is a consistent immediate Federalist.[15] On the other hand, Charles Hodge,[16] Michael McClymond, and Gerald McDermott[17] have all argued that Edwards was inconsistent in his theology, at times displaying federalism and at times displaying Augustinian realism. However, Oliver Crisp has recently put forth a new interpretation, which he calls the non-federalist immediate interpretation. Crisp claims that it is wrong to deny the federalist elements in Edwards and it is also wrong to deny Edwards's realist elements. From Edwards's Federalism, Crisp explains that "Adam stands in a particular relationship to his posterity as the first man" and from Edwards's realism Crisp explains "that there must be some ontological reality between Adam and his progeny being treated as one."[18] Thus, for Edwards they must form one metaphysical unity under a federal representative, Adam. At this point we must turn to Edward's metaphysics in order to understand how this is so.

First, we must understand that Edwards believes that God is continuously creating the world. That is that God continuously creates the world *ex nihilo* at each moment.

> God's upholding created substance, or causing its existence in each successive moment, is altogether equivalent to an immediate production out of nothing, at each moment, because its existence at this moment is not merely in part from God, but wholly from him; and not in any part or degree, from its antecedent existence.[19]

[19] *WJE* 3:402

This implies that the created world does not persist through time. If the created world does not persist through time, it is also the case that individual identities do not persist through time. Note what Edwards says in *Original Sin:*

> From these things it will clearly follow, that identity of consciousness depends wholly on a law of nature; and so, on the sovereign will and agency of God; and therefore that personal identity ... depends on an arbitrary divine constitution.[20]

[20] *WJE* 3:399

This means that John Doe at moment one (T_1) is not identical with John Doe at moment two (T_2), for Edwards it would be correct to say materially they are two completely different creations. However, this claim seems counterintuitive; it seems as though John Doe at T_1 is the same person as John Doe at T_2. Thankfully, Edwards has an answer as to why we can indeed say that John Doe at T_1 is the same person as John Doe at T_2; Edward's position is that identity persists over time because "God relates to me as one."[21] In *Original Sin* Edwards says,

[21] Holmes 2000, p. 141

> Some things, existing in different times and places, are treated by their Creator as one in one respect, and others in another; some are united for this communication, and others for that; but all according to the sovereign pleasure of the Fountain of all being and operation.[22]

[22] *WJE* 3:405

In other words, God regards John Doe at T_1 and T_2 as one being, even though materially they are not. Thus, metaphysically, it is true that John Doe at T_1 is the same person as John Doe at T_2. Edwards applies this same logic to the imputation of Christ's righteousness to humans. Edwards believes that "God regards the believers as one with Christ and so, ontologically, the believer is one with Christ."[23] The same can be said of the imputation of Adam's original sin to humanity,

[23] Holmes 2000, p. 149

> I am persuaded, no solid reason can be given, why God, who constitutes all other created union or oneness, according to his pleasure... may not establish a constitution whereby the natural posterity of Adam, proceeding from him, much as the buds and branches from the stock or root of a tree, should be treated as one with him, for the derivation, either of righteousness and communion in rewards, or of the loss of righteousness and consequent corruption and guilt.[24]

[24] *WJE* 3:405

In other words, God regards humans as one with Adam and so, ontologically, humans are one with Adam. So it is the case that original sin can justly be imputed to humans because metaphysically original sin is not only Adam's sin, it is ours as well.

Thus far we have seen that Edwards believes that humans need redemption because all of humanity has original sin. This original sin is due to humanity's metaphysical oneness with Adam. Now we turn to our second topic, Latino theology.

Latino Theology

Latino theology is a broad subject, which will vary greatly based upon the context in which it is done. For instance, Latino Catholic and Protestant theology will be very different. Also, Latino liberation theology from theologians like Leonardo Boff will be quite different from Latino constructive theology from theologians like Samuel Escobar. Finally, there will also be a great difference based upon where the theologian is working. Someone who is a Latino living in a majority Latino culture like Colombia will have a theology that differs greatly from a Latino living an a minority Latino culture like the United States.[25] It is this last scenario that I would like to examine, namely the theology of Justo Gonzalez, a Cuban-American theologian.

In his book *Mañana: Christian Theology from a Hispanic Perspective*, Gonzalez provides the reader with an example of what it looks like to do Latino theology as an immigrant in the United States. He says that Latino theology will place its emphasis on things that majority culture will likely not emphasize. For instance, Latino theology will be more sensitive to passages in the Bible that deal with poverty and oppression because of their experience as an oppressed minority in a majority culture. He also says that Latino theology will emphasize the unity between body and soul rather than emphasize the dichotomy between these two aspects of human nature. Although there are many other things that make Latino theology different from Western theology, in this paper I would like to focus on one: the emphasis on community.

Community

One way in which we see Gonzalez's emphasis on community is in his understanding of theology as a communal project. He calls theology as a communal project "Fuenteovejuna Theology." Gonzalez uses Lope de Vega's play "Fuenteovejuna" to explain what he means. In this play, the Spanish village of Fuenteovejuna is being oppressed by Don Fernan Gomez, a Spanish knight and commander in the army. The town comes together and rebels against this tyrant, killing him and placing his

[25] This scenario is personally important to me, being a first generation son of immigrants from Poland and Guatemala.

head on a pike as a banner of their freedom.[26] As King Ferdinand and Queen Isabella hear about the murder, they begin an inquisition into who killed the commander. Whenever the investigators ask *"Quien mato al comendador?"* (who killed the commander) the answer is always the same: *"Fuenteovejuan señor"* (Fuenteovejuna, my lord). The investigator becomes furious and tortures three hundred of the villagers, yet the answer to the question is still the same; the people always answer that Fuenteovejuna murdered the commander. Eventually Ferdinand and Isabella concede that "given such unanimity, there must have been just cause for the commander's death."[27] Gonzalez interprets this play as showing that the town could not think in terms of individuality; rather, it thought communally. An individual did not kill the commander, the whole village did. Gonzalez calls for a Fuenteovejuna theology, one that is not done individually but one that is done in community. He believes that this is a major contribution that Latino theology can bring to academic theology. Gonzalez claims that western theology is a task marked by individualism, but Latinos do not value individualism; rather, they value community. Gonzalez goes as far to say that Latinos value community so much that Spanish does not even have a word for privacy.[28]

[26] González 1990, p. 28

[27] González 1990, p. 29

[28] González 1990, p. 30

Evaluating Edwards's Theology

So far, we have given an overview of one aspect of Edwards's *hamartiology*. We also examined one aspect of Latino theology that is prominent in Justo Gonzalez's *Mañana*. We are now in a position to evaluate this aspect of Edwards's theology in light of Latino theology.

Why do Humans Need to be Saved—A Latino Evaluation

According to Edwards, humans are doubly guilty of sin; that is, humans sin and humans are born with original sin. Because of humanity's sinfulness, it needs redemption. This claim certainly is not unique to Edwards; in fact, Gonzalez would likely affirm the same claim. What is unique to Edwards is his non-federalist immediate imputation theory of original sin. As we have noted earlier, Edwards believes that sin is immediately imputed on to Adam's descendants because Adam's descendants are metaphysically in union with the head of the human race (Adam). What is interesting about this theory is that his metaphysical positions, namely his notion of continuous creation and lack of identity that persists over time, lead him to believe that humans are metaphysically united to Adam simply because God regards humans as one with Adam. In a dualist account of metaphysics this would seem ridiculous, at best it would be a legal fiction to consider Adam and humanity as one. However, in Edwards's idealism, whatever it is that God has an idea of is metaphysically true. Thus, if God actually considers Adam and humanity as metaphysically one, then their union is not fictive, it is metaphysically real.

This account of original sin being imputed to humanity through a metaphysical union with Adam fits well with Gonzalez's emphasis on community. As Gonzalez analyzes Lope de Vega's play "Fuenteovejuna" as a means for understanding Latino theology, he mentions that in this play no one individual is guilty of killing the commander; rather, it is the whole town that has killed the commander. In actuality, one person did kill the commander. However the village of "Fuenteovejuna" is so united and has such a sense of communal action that when they are asked *"Quien mato al comendador?"* (who killed the commander) the answer is always the same: *"Fuenteovejuan señor."* In the eyes of the village people this is the truth, it is not merely a fictive tale told to cover the guilt of the one who killed the commander.

In this play, the actions and guilt of one person are imputed onto the community; similarly in Edwards's understanding of original sin the actions and guilt of one person are imputed onto the community. Both Edwards and Gonzalez have a communal, rather than individualistic understanding of action and responsibility; thus we can say that in this respect Edward's theology is in line with Latino theology.

Conclusion

We began by saying that if Edwards is to be considered "America's theologian" then he must be able to speak constructively to the multiple American narratives, not only the Anglo-American narrative. I had claimed that one narrative that Edwards must be able to speak to if he is to be considered America's theologian is the Latino narrative. The Latino narrative, as seen in Gonzalez's *Mañana* emphasizes a communal understanding of reality. We examined Edward's hamartiology in light of this aspect of Latino theology and concluded that Edwards's theology is indeed compatible with it.

We have seen that despite being a theologian who worked in a European enlightenment context Edwards is also a theologian who can speak constructively to an Evangelical Latino-American context. It is my hope that more Evangelical Latino-American theologians will realize this and come to see Edwards as "America's theologian," a theologian who is capable of speaking to the manifold expressions of the American story including their own.

A Glimpse of the Brave New World of Discordant Voices into which Jonathan Edwards was Born

JONATHAN S. MARKO

Introduction

It is my intention in this chapter to give the reader a sense of the complex philosophical and theological world into which Jonathan Edwards was born (1703–1758). It would be foolhardy to try to lay out all of the rivulets of influence that converged potentially to produce the intellectual milieu that helped to form the young Edwards. Instead I would like to outline, in brief, two major conversations that had gained significant attention in the period leading up to Edwards's boyhood and beyond—the relationship of reason and revelation[1] and metaphysical freewill[2]—that did not run roughshod over his Puritan-Calvinist roots, but which challenged the stances of his forbearers.

So, I will point to the complexity and eclecticism of responses that faced the orthodox of Edwards's day in just two of the many on-going theological and philosophical conversations. It will be shown that these conversations were not battles between the so-called orthodox and a singular heterodox faction, or at least between two opposing traditions, as some histories might tend to present them.[3] Nothing is rarely that neat, though such well-read presentations have helped many readers gain traction in terms of what was at stake and important.

I hasten to add that these conversations and the positions striving for ascendancy were nothing new. There are perhaps new labels applied or a new weaving of old threads. In other words, during the Enlightenment some positions received more attention than they previously had. For instance, while scholarship focusing on the Enlightenment will often highlight the impact of the deists and, even more recently, the pantheists,[4] John Calvin was actively combatting them in their various forms, or at least some of their primary underlying premises, as did

[1] Turretin 1992; Muller 1992; Herbert 1937; Marko 2016; Tindal 1730; Marko 2012; Williams 1696; Strauss 1953; Strauss 1952

[2] Moreland and Craig 2003; Hobbes and Bramhall 1999; Hobbes 1654; Hobbes 1656; Marko 2010a; Clarke 1717; Collins 1717. For discussions concerning Calvinism's historical relationship to so-called libertarian and necessitarian or compatibilist thought, see: Muller 1995, pp. 251–78; Schreiner 1983, pp. 30–32; Marko 2010b, pp. 41–60; Crisp 2015, chap. 5; Crisp 2014, chap. 3; Peterson et al. 2013, chap. 8

[3] Stephen 1962, Stephen does make a distinction between "constructive deism" and "critical deism" though there is a significant simplifying of the narrative; Randall Jr. 1976, pp. 285–94; Livingston 2006, chap. 2; Peterson et al. 2013

[4] E.g., Sullivan 1982

⁵ Schreiner 1983, pp. 16–22

theologians down through the ages.[5] There is nothing new under the sun. Discussions and debates over the relationship of revelation and reason and our so-called free will in light of a sovereign deity are to be numbered among the ancient ones; but, in those two areas, there were some interesting discussions and the gaining of more space in the Christianized world by voices that had been significantly muted prior to the Enlightenment.

Reason and Revelation

Of Handmaidens and Queens

Theology is the queen of the sciences and philosophy is her hand-maiden. This hierarchical relationship can be mapped onto revelation, in our case Scripture, and human reason (abstractly considered as the power or faculty of reasoning). In the early Enlightenment era, Reformed theologian Francis Turretin writes this about the relationship between the two: "Rather the question is whether it [the human reasoning faculty] is the first principle from which the doctrines of the faith are proved; or the foundation upon which they are built, so that we must hold to be false in things of the faith what the natural light or human reason cannot comprehend."[6] For Turretin, the rest of the orthodox Reformed, Lutherans, and so on, Scripture is the first principle and foundation of theology. It is our job to apply our reasoning abilities to Scripture, prayerfully with guidance and assistance from the Holy Spirit, to understand it in its own context. Furthermore, we are to see to it that we do not set passage against passage and author against author and allow for (obvious) logical contradictions in our theology. While Scripture will often make assertions that we would not otherwise believe or even conclude with our biblically unassisted or naked and (now) corrupt reason, it may also tell us things that we cannot mentally reconcile. For instance, that one cannot envision a non-misdirecting analogy for the doctrine of the Holy Trinity—one God who is three persons, each of which is fully God—has been the topic of many interesting conversations in innumerable catechism classes and undergraduate, introductory theology courses.

In short, in our approach to Scripture, we are to be prepared eventually to have what we would otherwise think of as "reasonable" to be overturned. That is not, however, to throw reason out. Reason has its place as a subordinate. In fact, it was not Thomas Aquinas' intention to show theology and the Bible as reasonable in his "five ways" by which he could rationally prove the existence of God, but rather it was his intention to show that our human reason, though harmed, was still sound enough to conclude the same as Scripture: God exists. This is

⁶ Turretin 1992, 1:24. Turretin gives a helpful breakdown of the different senses of the term "reason" prior to the quotation given above. There he notes that the term can be taken subjectively, as we have done above, or objectively, "for the natural light both externally presented and internally impressed upon the mind by which reason is disposed to the forming of certain conceptions and the eliciting of conclusions concerning God and divine things." In both instances reason can be considered pre- and post-fall.

important for Aquinas to argue as he would proceed to utilize reason and philosophy in his theologizing.[7]

"Scripture is our supreme authority" has been the position of the orthodox. But we still need reason as an assistant to respectfully and dutifully present God's message in its glory and utmost purity. Of course, how far reason should go has been differently determined by the orthodox traditions. But in the Enlightenment era, discordant voices became louder than they had been in recent centuries, in some cases calling for a different understanding of the queen's authority, and in others, calling for a new queen outright. In the Enlightenment, during the rise of natural religion, the so-called deists are often cast as the heterodox faction opposing the orthodox. In what follows, however, I would like to show how even those that we call deists disagree on the precise relationship of revelation and reason.

The Rise of Natural Religion and the So-Called Deists

In the narratives focusing on the rise of natural religion in England, one thinker consistently is found at the beginning of the tale: Edward, Lord Herbert of Cherbury (1583–1648).[8] He was an English contemporary of René Descartes who never received the attention of his French counterpart. He is known today mostly as the "Father of Deism," a moniker bequeathed upon him by the historians of philosophy. In his 1624 work, *De Veritate*, Lord Herbert speaks at length of common notions, in one part noting: "Common notions are so called because they are understood by all normal men, so long as their objects, whether they be things, terms or signs, remain constant."[9] It was Lord Herbert's conclusion that all *normal* humans have faculties associated with particular truths and then when confronted by these truths these internal faculties spring to activity and alert their persons to the truths before them.[10] He goes on to list five common, religious notions that all normal humans have: 1) there is a supreme God; 2) the sovereign deity ought to be worshipped; 3) virtue and piety are the most important aspect of our religious obeisance; 4) we must expiate our sins by repentance; and 5) there is reward or punishment after this life.[11] While Lord Herbert still admits special revelation, these common notions—again, common to all *normal* humans—are that by which we judge whether or not a particular alleged revelation is such: "I value these so highly that the book, religion, and prophet which adheres most closely to them is the best."[12] For Lord Herbert, these five common, religious notions serve as the foundation of all true religion.[13]

The importance owed to Lord Herbert in the narrative at hand is not a denouncement of Scripture but the claim that God has endowed us with commonly-held faculties to judge the legitimacy of purported

[7] Muller 1992

[8] See: Marko 2012, chap. 5; Marko 2016. Both focus on the common figures and connections found in histories of philosophy covering the rise or natural religion.

[9] Herbert 1937, p. 126

[10] Herbert 1937, pp. 122–23; cf. (Marko, 2016, pp. 43–44)

[11] Herbert 1937, pp. 291–302. This succinct interpretation of the five common, religious notions is taken verbatim from Marko 2016, p. 45.

[12] Herbert 1937, pp. 289–91

[13] Herbert 1937, pp. 303, 312–13

Fig. 12: Edward, Lord Herbert of Cherbury (1583–1648)

[13] Cf. Tindal 1730, p. 59; Marko 2012, chap. 5

[14] Leo Strauss has helped popularize the idea that many philosophers throughout history, especially those that could be persecuted for their irreligious conclusions, had to write in a way such to mask their true thoughts—which would only be determined by reading-in-between-the-lines—with seemingly orthodox assertions. See: (Strauss, 1953); (Strauss, 1952)

[14] Williams 1696, pp. 19–20

[15] Williams 1696, p. 28. Williams steers clear of fashioning anything as an absurdity that might be of significant import like the doctrine of the Holy Trinity. That is one doctrine, however, for which we cannot form an idea, even an analogous one. Cf. (Marko, 2012, chaps. 3 & 4)

revelation. In fact, if Lord Herbert had been more detailed about the five common, religious notions, one might conclude that he was favoring Christianity. But that human reason stands in the arbiter's chair of revelation, at least, initially, surely gave many readers pause. Inferring from what has been so far conveyed, while revelation might assert some things reason could not determine itself, on particular issues it is the rule and foundation of religion.

While Lord Herbert is found at the beginning of the tale, one of the clearest articulations of so-called deism, Matthew Tindal's *Christianity as Old as the Creation,* was not published until 100 years after *De Veritiate.* The former work is sometimes called the "Deist's Bible." In it, Tindal proclaims that special revelation, namely Scripture, and human reason agree. Though not asserting (to my knowledge) that revelation might assist human reason, he at least does not say that it cannot. He does, however, seem to advance the idea that any revelation that is found to be "unreasonable" cannot be considered as being from God.[13] It is that stance that goes even further than Lord Herbert was willing to assert. In the end, God-given reason, operating at its best, is the rule and foundation of religion. True revelation will conform to it. God had made it thus. Reason confirms Christianity and Scripture as being reasonable and thus being divine. Of course, one could take Tindal as being insincere, and thus in truth dismissing revelation outright and covertly making an argument that no revelation should be accepted as such.[14]

So far I have just outlined in brief three different types of deism: the Lord Herbert variety and two different interpretations of Tindal. The first makes reason queen in some areas. The second—the "sincere" reading of Tindal—makes reason queen and revelation the handmaiden. The third has executed the true queen.

There is, at least, one more type of deist to discuss when considering the relationship of reason and revelation. In Stephen Williams's *An Account of the Growth of Deism in England,* he points out the many reasons for heterodoxy in England. But of interest to our purposes here, in that book he points out a group (for which he has much sympathy) that appears to accept, at least, most (biblical) revelation as being such; however, they will either not accept revelation as such that teaches incomprehensible doctrines or they refuse to accept interpretations that result in incomprehensible doctrines. This group complains, "Many Doctrines (*say these*) are made necessary to Salvation, which 'tis impossible to believe, because they are in their nature Absurdities."[14] One from this group, defining what a so-called absurdity is, identifies it with anything for which he could not "form to my self an Idea."[15] Again, while such a rule does not necessarily exclude any biblical passage, if one is acceptable, it does rule out certain theological conclusions or interpretations one might make. In short, their position is that one should be prepared eventually to have one's "reasonable" beliefs and opinions overturned, and to believe something that one has never considered before, with the exception of that for which one cannot form an idea. Belief in that situation is impossible.

Impact Summary

These differences that I just outlined within the so-called deists on just one major issue, the relationship of reason and revelation, is indicative of the reality behind the simplified or "smoother" histories with which many readers are confronted. And this is simply on one of the many "sides" of the reason and revelation debate. The era into which Edwards was born and its thinkers had to wrestle with a cacophony of voices claiming truth.

Freedom of the Will

Older Orthodox Model

Many theology students, especially self-professed Calvinists, are surprised when they learn that many of its forbearers prior to Jonathan Edwards do not fall into the definition of a compatilibilist or soft determinist but often are described as sharing some commonalities with libertarians.[16] The issue of regeneration aside, Francis Turretin says this about concursus and the liberty of second causes:

> These two things we derive most clearly from Scriptures: that the providence of God concurs with all second causes and especially with the human will; yet the contingency and liberty of the will remain unimpaired. But how these two things can consist with each other, no mortal can in this life perfectly understand. Nor should it seem a cause for wonder, since he has a thousand ways (to us incomprehensible) of concurring with our will, insinuating himself into us and turning our hearts, so that by acting freely as we will, we still do nothing besides the will and determination of God.[17]

In short, he is affirming that human agents have potencies to multiple effects—they are not determined to do anything vis-à-vis the created order, and thus they have liberty—yet God has foreordained all things that come to pass and concurs with even our free or contingent actions. To the perplexed reader he admits his own perplexity: "Although I cannot understand how these can be mutually connected together, yet the thing itself is (which is certain from another source, i.e., from the word) not either to be called in question or wholly denied."[18] Yet, during the Enlightenment, we appear to have varied strident attempts to

[16] I have taken the following definitions from Moreland and Craig, "Free Will and Determinism." *Determinism (general)*: view that for every event that happens, there are conditions such that, given them, nothing else could have happened. For every event that happens, its happening was caused or necessitated by prior factors, the event in question had to occur. *Hard Determinism (more specific)*: denies the existence of free will (as understood by libertarians) and agrees with the libertarians that determinism and free will are incompatible. *Soft Determinism or Compatibilism (more specific)*: holds that freedom and determinism are compatible with each other, and thus the truth of determinism does not eliminate freedom. Free will or freedom, simply, must be redefined differently than their hard determinist and libertarian counterparts. *Libertarianism*: freedom necessary for responsible action is not compatible with determinism.

[17] Turretin 1992, 1:511

[18] Turretin 1992, 1:512

convince the interested, literate public of particular ways of reconciling human free will and divine sovereignty.

Freewill Debates

The first major, published series of exchanges in the Enlightenment free will debates came from the pens of Thomas Hobbes (1588–1679) and John Bramhall (1594–1663). It is much too complex to outline in detail this debate that took place in the 1650s. Nonetheless, Hobbes, striving to summarize their respective positions up to the then-present, writes:

> ...[the debate] between two persons [Hobbes and Bramhall] who both maintain that Men are Free to Do as they Will, and to Forbear as they Will. The things they dissent in are, that the one [Hobbes] holdeth, That it is not in a Mans Power now, to choose the Will he shall have anon; That Chance produceth nothing; That all Events and Actions have their Necessary Causes; That the Will of God make the Necessity of all things. The other on the contrary maintaineth, That not onely the Man is Free to choose what he will Do, but the Will also to choose what it shall Will; That when a Man willeth a good Action, Gods Will concurreth with his, else not; That the Will may choose whether it will Will or not; That many things come to pass without Necessity that that thing shall be, in as much as God seeth no the future as in its Causes, but as present. In sum, they adheare both of them to the Scripture; but one of them [Bramhall] is a learned School-Divine, the other a man [Hobbes] that doth not much admire that kind of learning.[19]

In short, according to Hobbes the actions of humans and their corresponding "choices" are all necessary. That is, what transpires is directly the result of the chain of events or causes preceding and bearing upon the acting agent. Thus, given a particular past, an agent will inevitably follow a certain course of actions. Analogously speaking, humans are part of the universal clockwork, the motions of which are predetermined and which happen, in nature, in a necessary order and according to natural laws. According to Bramhall, our actions and decisions (the issue of the conversion of sinners aside)[20] are not necessary but free. One's past history up to a particular decision could very well influence what one does next, but it does not necessitate it. In summary, Thomas Hobbes thought that we have potency to one effect at all times, and Bramhall thought that we, at least generally, have potency to multiple effects.

There are a few issues to note regarding this debate. First, and arguably, Hobbes and Bramhall exert themselves in their attempts to make their positions on human free will, in light of our sovereign God, reasonable or as comprehensible as possible. Second, this is more of a debate about metaphysics than it is about soteriology. This was not the Calvinists versus the Arminians. In fact, while Jonathan Edwards is

Fig. 13: Thomas Hobbes (1588–1679)

[19] Hobbes 1656, preface

[20] Hobbes 1656, p. 2

often taken as being metaphysically closer to Hobbes on the question of free will, in my mind Francis Turretin, one of Edwards's Reformed predecessors, believes that Christians have potencies to multiple effects. And finally, according to Vere Chappell, Hobbes further popularized the idea that the libertarian view of the will is that it is random or arbitrary in its choice.[21] Libertarians were compelled to distance themselves from this reading and disabuse their readers of this connection.

This last point is demonstrated in the continuation of the liberty-necessity debates in the course of the exchange between two formidable opponents of the next generation: Samuel Clarke (1675–1729), the libertarian proponent, and Anthony Collins (1676–1729), the necessitarian proponent. Clarke takes a standard libertarian stance that the human will is self-moving and expresses perplexity at Collins's identification of that position with the one maintaining that the human will is arbitrary or random.[22] He claims that Collins's identification amounts to "that there is no Middle between *Necessity* and *Absolute Indifferency*."[23] Libertarian freedom is neither fish nor fowl in Clarke's mind. Admittedly, the conceptual difficulty that Collins and perhaps Hobbes, and many other necessitarians have when it comes to what most libertarians claim, is an inability to comprehend those claims. In our world of analogies, one does seem to have recourse only to mechanical necessity or the seeming randomness of a rolling di. *Via negativa* theology is not very satisfying, but that is what, conceptually-speaking, Clarke's brand of libertarianism becomes.

Impact Summary

There are a few things that are worth drawing attention to in considering this brief rehearsal of the early Enlightenment free will debates. While Edwards apparently goes on to be considered as a type of necessitarian, Hobbes and Collins, the earlier defenders of that type of position were considered heterodox, though not only for their positions on metaphysical free will. That is not to say Bramhall or Clarke were the "poster boys" of orthodoxy. And so, Edwards is perhaps one of the first major, generally-considered-orthodox theologians who appropriated a necessitarian metaphysic. On a related note, as already alluded to above, one must be careful about notionally connecting Calvinism and necessitarianism (or its modern-day counterpart, compatibilism). We even see some of the best minds promulgating this erroneous connection: "Calvinists hold that only by affirming such a strong sense of sovereignty can the majesty of God be sufficiently affirmed. Any view that allows some decisions about the course of events to be made by humans and not by God deprives God of glory and is demeaning to God."[24] In other words, these thinkers assume "Calvinism" and

[21] Hobbes and Bramhall 1999, p. 39n45; Hobbes 1654, p. 73; Marko 2010a, p. 80

[22] Clarke 1717, pp. 6, 12; cf. Marko 2010a, p. 90

[23] Clarke 1717, pp. 36–37; cf. Marko 2010a, p. 90

Fig. 14: Anthony Collins (1676–1729)

[24] Peterson et al. 2013, pp. 162; Cf. 163; 175n4; 175n5

"contingency in our decisions" have part ways. Recall, Turretin claims God's sovereignty in the strongest sense and human free choice (again, issues of conversion aside) are both somehow true.

Conclusion

Historical accounts are only as neat and orderly or as chaotic as the historian desires to present them. In this chapter it was my aim to give the reader a taste of the complexity of the philosophical and theological world into which Jonathan Edwards was born. In the on-going conversations regarding the relationship of reason and revelation, it is hardly the case that during the rise of natural religion it was the orthodox thinkers pitted against the deists. Those labels are too simplistic. In short order it was shown that the so-called deists did not precisely agree on the answer to the question of the relationship. And, when it comes to metaphysical discussions regarding human free will, the various positions did not find themselves organized into two neat groups. In fact, one at the time might reel at the suggestion that either the necessitarians or libertarians involved in the free will debates could be labeled "orthodox." But more importantly, it was not simply a battle between "Hobbesian" necessitarians and "Bramhallian" libertarians, though those are the ones slugging it out center-stage on occasion. What is more, it is not always clear that the interlocutors completely understood one another.

Jonathan Edwards and Caring for the Book of Nature

ROBERT BOSS

Jonathan Edwards's typological worldview, which permeated his preaching and writing, carries profound environmental implications for the twenty-first century. In a day in which the scientific worldview has stripped nature of its divine voice, Evangelicals are left with little or no natural theology. Yet Psalm 19 speaks of the quiet beauty of nature where the word of God is ubiquitous, and Wisdom says, "Go to the ant, O sluggard; consider her ways, and be wise" (Proverbs 6:6 ESV). Concerning nature as a word of God, Edwards wrote:

> For such a system (or Bible) of the word of God is as much the work of God as any other of his works, the effect of the power, wisdom and contrivance of a God whose wisdom is unsearchable and whose nature and ways are past finding out. And as the system of nature and the system of revelation are both divine works, so both are in different senses a divine word. Both are the voice of God to intelligent creatures, a manifestation and declaration of himself to mankind. Man's reason was given him that he might know God and might be capable of discerning the manifestations he makes of himself in the effects and external expressions and emanations of the divine perfections.[1]

If the care of creation is not merely a matter of conserving natural resources and keeping the planet in good order but also preserving the revelatory Book of Nature, environmental stewardship gains an entirely new level of urgency. Edwards's natural theology provides a distinctly Christian argument for stewardship and care of the creation. Edwards challenges humans to a renewed encounter with nature and a devotional use of creation, exemplified in his "Personal Narrative" and "Images of Divine Things," which discovers divine wisdom and the God who is near.[2]

Though Edwards expressed concern that many people would consider his devotional views overenthusiastic and groundless, he was undaunted. When considering the twenty–eight years that Edwards

Fig. 15: The ant

[1] "Miscellanies" no. 1340, *WJE* 23:374

[2] Alister McGrath notes Edwards as an example of a theologian who employs "affective imagination" in a correlation of doctrine and natural theology: "...Edwards...perhaps America's greatest Christian theologian, developed an approach to theology which at the very least safeguarded the affective aspects of faith (many would say emphasized those aspects), especially in his reflections on the world of nature...As is clear from Edwards's approach, a Christian spirituality is intertwined with and informed by a Christian theology, even if their points of focus are not the same" (McGrath, 2016, pp. 163–65).

spent on the "Images" notebook, a life–long pursuit, one must hope that future scholars will build upon Edwards's radically theocentric worldview in which the commonplaces of daily life become re-enchanted with scriptural meaning.

Such building upon the foundation laid by Edwards will not require innovation on the part of future theologians. Rather, a return to some of the concerns of the past will suffice to further strengthen this profoundly Christian reinscripturated worldview.[3] The most obvious areas to which Edwards's emblematic worldview can contribute are creation care and the right use of creation. A reconsideration of Edwards's emblematic theology casts both of these issues in a new light. Edwards wrote,

> 70. If we look on these shadows of divine things as the voice of God, purposely, by them, teaching us these and those spiritual and divine things, to show of what excellent advantage it will be, how agreeably and clearly it will tend to convey instruction to our minds, and to impress things on the mind, and to affect the mind. By that we may as it were hear God speaking to us. Wherever we are and whatever we are about, we may see divine things excellently represented and held forth, and it will abundantly tend to confirm the Scriptures, for there is an excellent agreement between these things and the Holy Scriptures.[4]

Three centuries later, an Edwardsean natural theology may experience a renaissance through invitations such as *The Creation: An Appeal to Save Life on Earth.* Written by famed Harvard sociobiologist E.O. Wilson as a letter to a Southern Baptist pastor, *The Creation* describes the planet's ecological crisis and extends a hand to Baptists and Evangelicals in hopes that they will join forces with the scientific community to save the Earth.

Despite leaving the faith during his college studies, Wilson now desires that science and religion set aside their differences and unite for the common good. He makes a very interesting statement at the end of his first chapter: "I already know much of the religious argument on behalf of the Creation, and would like to learn more."[5] Wilson suggests that early in the history of humanity a wrong turn was taken, an attempt to "ascend from Nature instead of to Nature."[6] The "ascent to Nature" is defined as an acknowledgment of our natural heritage, and a compliance with "the gravitational pull of the natural world on our spirit, and on our souls."[7] Wilson argues that the teachings of Scripture are inadequate in this area. Humans sense a responsibility to environmental stewardship, but no explanation has been available due to inadequate education and the explosion of biological knowledge. Wilson's answer is that nature should be recognized as "opening up a broad pathway to the heart of science itself," and that humanity's fate is intertwined with the fate of the creation.[8] The solution he envisions is an *Encyclopedia of Life* which catalogs each species according to genetic

---

[3] Along with Edwards, McGrath points to the work of Catalan scholar Raymond de Sebonde (1385-1436). Posthumously published in 1438, Sebonde's *Theologia naturalis seu Liber creaturarum* (Natural Theology) is an instance of an integration of the "two books" of God's revelation. McGrath notes that the concern of the Protestant reformers to translate the book of Scripture into the vernacular echoes the value of the book of nature which was easily accessible to the common man of little or no literacy (McGrath, 2016, p. 80).

[4] "Images" no. 70, *WJE* 11:74. Raymond de Sebonde's thought was popular through the 16th and 17th centuries (Manning, 2013, pp. 57–58). Appeals to the common man through natural theology were both popular and effective with some 16th century Radical Reformers (Packull, 1986, pp. 53-55). Anabaptist Hans Hut noted that Jesus taught the Gospel to gardeners through trees, fishermen through fish, carpenters through building, goldsmiths through smelting, housewives through dough, vinekeepers through vineyards and the fruit of the vine, tailors through mending cloth, merchants through pearls, reapers through the harvest, woodsmen through axe and trees, shepherds through sheep, potters through clay, stewards and overseers through accounting, pregnant women through birth, threshers through winnowing, and butchers through slaughter (Hut, 1994, p. 69). Hut's premise was: "For the whole world with all the creatures is a book which in our actions is like what is read in a written book. The elect from the beginning of the world until Moses studied this book of all creatures and gained understanding from it" (Hut, 1994, p. 71). From this quote Hut exhibits a sure dependence upon Raymond de Sebonde's *Natural Theology* (Rupp, 1961, pp. 508–09).

[5] Wilson 2006, p. 8

[6] Wilson 2006, p. 13

[7] Wilson 2006, p. 13

[8] Wilson 2006, pp. 13–14

code, anatomy, behavior, life cycle, and environmental role.[9] Each species' incredibly complicated evolutionary history deserves to be celebrated by not only scientists but also historians and poets. This is his "compelling moral argument" for saving the creation.[10]

Edwards's sermon on Romans 8:22 would most certainly give Wilson and friends reason to celebrate—a beautiful creation that groans, suffers, and bleeds under the greedy excesses and abuses of humanity is a concern shared by both Wilson and Edwards:

> Thus the light of the sun is improved. The sun rises day after day upon the nations that dwell upon the face of the earth. But how do they improve it, but to serve sin and Satan by it, to serve their pride, and their covetousness, and their sensuality? They work by the light of the sun all their days for no other purposes. God has given the earth to them for an habitation to them, but they improve it to make it a stage of all manner of wickedness. And the sea is improved for transportation to convey what may gratify men's lusts. And to the same purpose do they improve the air that they breathe, and all the fruits that the earth yields to 'em year after year. They are not improved for God, the giver of them, but only for their lusts. For this end they make the innocent brute creatures serve them, the oxen that plow their fields, the horses they ride on, and the sheep and silkworm that yield them clothing and ornaments. They improve these things to serve and pamper their pride. And for those ends they improve the lives of the brute animals. They kill them to be a sacrifice to their lusts: the many thousands and millions of them that are slain every day, the greater part of them are killed only to serve men's lusts: the beasts and birds, they bring forth and nurse up their young to be a prey to men's lusts.[11]

The right use of creation, though defined differently by materialist Wilson and spiritualist Edwards, tends toward a common goal—the proper conservation and care of creation. This concern was not unique to Edwards, but was shared widely by other early Evangelicals, including John Bunyan and Richard Baxter. Along with Edwards, they viewed the spiritual use of creation as the highest use—as an object of meditation, guided by Scripture.[12] The early Evangelical poetic celebration of creation as a voice of God is agreeable to Wilson's "compelling moral argument" for saving the creation. Jonathan Edwards's radically theocentric worldview and theology provides a narrow ecological footprint, which is yet wide enough for both environmentalists and Evangelicals to share.

[9] http://eol.org

[10] Wilson 2006, pp. 119–23

[11] Sermon no. 445 on Rom. 8:22, *WJEO* 52. The shared theme of creation's suffering gains a Christological focus in Hut's "Gospel of All Creatures" (Hut, 1994, p. 71).

[12] For a more full treatment of Edwards's typology and natural theology, see *God-Haunted World: The Elemental Theology of Jonathan Edwards* (Boss, 2015). For an excellent discussion of the "Book of Nature" from a Roman Catholic point of view, see (Tanzella-Nitti, 2005). Fr. Giuseppe Tanzella-Nitti, Professor of Fundamental Theology at the Pontifical University of the Holy Cross, Rome, is currently writing a large volume dedicated to the historical heritage of the Metaphor of the Two Books, including its theological value, from the ancient literature to the contemporary epoch.

Jonathan Edwards through the Eyes of His Children

ZACHARY HOPKINS

In keeping with J.I. Packer's metaphor of the Puritans as the Redwoods in the forest of church history, one could easily argue that Jonathan Edwards stands prominently among the grandest of them all.[1] Although he would have known himself primarily as a pastor, Edwards is remembered mostly for the many fine written works he produced in his brief fifty-four-year life including prominent titles such as *Freedom of the Will, Religious Affections,* and *The Life & Diary of David Brainerd.* This list is abbreviated, to say the least, but nonetheless suggests that scholarly interest in Jonathan Edwards has focused more on his works than his person.

[1] Packer 2010, p. 11

Perhaps the greatest benefit to understanding the works of this great American Puritan is not only to understand him in a historical and theological context, but a personal one as well. Edwards was a scientist, philosopher, theologian, pastor, and educator among many things; but at the end of the day, he was still a man, and a family man at that. By seeking to understand Edwards the man, greater depth of understanding and appreciation will be shown from the study of this important figure. In order to contribute greater understanding to his life, this paper seeks to parse the family life of Edwards through a detailed look at each of his eleven children. This will confirm that among the many areas in which Edwards is a commendable model of ministry, family life must not be excluded.

Unfortunately, Edwards is often cast in a particular light that might suggest his roles as husband and father were subservient to academician and author. There are many misconceptions regarding his personal disciplines that have led many to conclude that Edwards was nothing more than an aloof intellect who truly wasn't fit for pastoral ministry (thus, justifying his ejection) and stands as a poor model of ministry to his family. The foundation of this misunderstanding is based on the reports of his first biographer Samuel Hopkins. Of Edwards's rigorous

Fig. 16: Samuel Hopkins (1721–1803)

[2] Hopkins 1765, p. 40

[3] Murray 1987, pp. 185–86

Fig. 17: Sarah Pierrepont Edwards (1710–58)

[4] Dodds 1971; Piper 2004, pp. 55–78

[5] Marsden 2003, p. 321

[6] Marsden 2003, p. 321

[7] The most well known objective accounts of the Edwards household come from Massachusetts pastor Joseph Emerson, early biographer Samuel Hopkins, and family friend George Whitefield. Emerson said of the household that it was "the most agreeable family I was ever acquainted with. Much of the presence of God here" (Marsden, 2003, p. 342). Concerning Sarah, Hopkins wrote "she had an excellent way of governing her children" (Piper, 2004, p. 64). After staying with the Edwards family Whitefield would say, "Felt wonderful satisfaction in being at the house of Mr. Edwards. He is a Son himself, and hath also a Daughter of Abraham for his wife. A sweeter couple I have not yet seen" (Piper, 2004, p. 67).

schedule Hopkins explains, "Though he was of a tender and delicate constitution, few students are capable of close application more hours in a day than he. He commonly spends thirteen hours every day in his study."[2] The question has naturally been asked: how could a man who seemingly locked himself away for the majority of every day be considered a proper model for any ministry, most especially to his own family?

Many biographers since Hopkins have tried to account for the intense schedule in light of his other responsibilities in an attempt to ease the impression that Edwards was impersonal and aloof. Iain Murray gives several reasons why the infamous *thirteen hours* should not automatically exclude Edwards as a worthy model of life and ministry.[3] First, the time spent in his study was by no means secluded. Edwards' study was open to his wife Sarah and children, but also to his congregation. He thought he could be more effective if his parishioners were allowed easy access to him, rather than he trying to constantly visit them. Second, his hospitality, although mostly at the hands of Sarah's efforts, was reputable. Most notable was his practice of seeing guests off by riding out some distance with them from the Northampton parsonage. Third, although a man of extraordinary brilliance, he was also competent in commons affairs such as business and managing the home in the absence of his wife. Finally, his relationship with his children suggests that they did not understand their father to be aloof or remote as they enjoyed a healthy relationship common in the time of colonial life. It is on this last reason that this paper will focus in order to counter the notion that Edwards was an absent or aloof father.

Edwards' model of parenting kept with his biblical understanding of male headship where he understood the father to keep rule and order in the home. However, the demands on his time necessitated that he trust the daily operations of the family to his faithful wife Sarah. Biographer Samuel Hopkins spoke of Sarah as a "deputy husband" with regard to the significance of her role in the upkeep of the household. Much has been written about the wonderful marriage of Jonathan and Sarah Edwards, especially in regard to their roles in the home.[4] For example, there can be no doubt that the greater burden of childrearing was given to Sarah, but it should also be noted that Jonathan played a significant role as the head of the home when it came to the need for disciplining in order to establish patterns of obedience.[5] Hopkins recalls that Jonathan's fatherly discipline was rigorous, bringing the children into submission, but with a stern calmness that did not necessitate violence.[6] Because of this, parental authority was established that allowed Sarah to manage a home of delightfully obedient children. Regardless of the ratio of responsibility, the Edwards home was well managed, which is a fact well attested to by several witnesses.[7]

Contrary to popular opinion, Jonathan Edwards was not successful in ministry and publication at the expense of his family; rather, his family thrived under his pursuit of godliness that he modeled before them in daily life. As a shepherd and priest in his own home, he exercised his spiritual authority as father and head of the home in several ways.[8] For example, the study was more than a private space; it was a personal sanctuary where prayer and writing were combined into a place of daily worship.[9] This discipline was set before the family's eyes as a model for them to follow. Additionally, the regular practice of family worship twice a day where Edwards would attend to family prayers, oversee the reading of Scripture, and examine his children by means of catechism according to their age and capacity for understanding reportedly took place within Edwards' study. The most intentional time that he spent with his family at large outside of religious discipline was the daily hour after the evening meal. This was an hour, not for family worship, but of conversation where the whole family participated, and Jonathan could make specific inquiries into the lives of each of his children.[10] Finally, like all Puritan families, the week was established around the Lord's Day. In preparation for this, the family would cease all their secular business by sundown on Saturday evening and then join together in worship (psalm singing and prayers) in order to sanctify the Sabbath in their lives.[11]

A final conclusion can be drawn regarding Edwards as a parent that is obviously connected to his larger theological worldview. The most fundamental thing to understand about Edwards is that he did not see life in this world as an end in itself and his parenting reflects it. The greatest love a parent can give to their children is to commend the love of Jesus Christ and the eternal life which faith in Him affords. Edwards would argue that life was too short to do anything that did not aid in preparation for eternity.[12] Therefore, there are two discernible themes that resound through the lives of his children: religious commitment, and the brevity of life. The remainder of this paper will turn to each one of his eleven children to demonstrate from their own experiences how their father's influence on them is sufficient evidence for affirming him as a godly father. By tracing the children's history in relation to their father and examining primary sources that provide insight into their relationships, this conclusion will have strong evidence.

Sarah "Sally" Edwards Parsons

The first of many covenant blessings came to Jonathan and Sarah just past their one-year anniversary. Sarah, or Sally[13] as the family knew her, was seven years old during the Northampton and Connecticut Valley awakening.[14] Edwards himself believed that Sarah had come to

[8] In traditional Puritan fashion Edwards understood the home to be a model of patriarchal governance in line with Christ's headship over the church. The biblical reality was that God, in His wisdom had designed social hierarchies whereby some would rule and others would be subject to their authority. In his own home, he exercised spiritual leadership as a model of godliness (Marsden, 2003, p. 187).

[9] Murray 1987, pp. 143, 145

[10] Winslow 1972, p. 128. The hour that was spent with the family included Edwards "relaxed into cheerful and animated conversation" where he "entered truly into the feelings and concerned of his children." These important times served to unify the family with love for one another: a reality tested through many trials (Murray, 1987, p. 186).

[11] Murray 1987, p. 187

[12] Winslow 1972, p. 133

[13] 8/25/1728–5/15/1805 (76 years). Married to Elihu Parsons, a local and prosperous man on 6/11/1750 at 21 years old. Their wedding was just eight days before the council was convened to dismiss Edwards from his pastorate at Northampton.

[14] Winslow 1972, p. 164

[15] Marsden 2003, p. 214

[16] Marsden 2003, pp. 214, 251

[17] Marsden 2003, pp. 307, 317, 322

[18] Moody 2007, p. 162

[19] Marsden 2003, p. 307

[20] Winslow 1972, p. 218

[21] Murray 1987, p. 401; Marsden 2003, pp. 363, 391; Winslow 1972, p. 313

[22] Letter no. 33, WJE 16:95

[23] Marsden 2003, pp. 207, 214, 327

[24] 4/6/1730–2/14/1747 (17 years). Jerusha passed away after nursing David Brainerd during his failing health. Their rumored betrothal is a debated point of history but the evidence is circumstantial and speculative at best. Biographer Winslow actually records their betrothal without any evidence(Winslow, 1972, p. 236). Iain Murray argues that their relationship was spiritual, and that this is the correct way to understand Brainerd's desire to be with Jerusha in heaven. Additionally, Murray points out that the reason why Jerusha attended to Brainerd was because she was the oldest available nurse because her mother was busy attending to newborn Elizabeth (Murray, 1987, pp. 309–10). Brainerd's words upon seeing Jerusha for the last time as the primary reason for speculation, in addition to her father's decision to lay their graves next to each other.

[25] Marsden 2003, pp. 128, 251, 323

[26] Marsden 2003, p. 341

[27] Marsden 2003, p. 224

[28] Marsden 2003, p. 322

saving faith around the age of ten or eleven.[15] Even as a young girl she was advanced in religion which no doubt provided her comfort during the many times she suffered with sickness.[16] As was common of the children, Sarah often accompanied her father on trips to various locations including Boston in 1743, Long Island in 1746, and New Haven in 1744 and 1747.[17] Especially noteworthy is the trip to Boston when on the road she and her father rode alongside Thomas Clap, the 'Old Light' Rector of Yale.[18] We can imagine that Sarah would have listened as her father discussed the nature of revival and shared his thoughts published in *The Distinguishing Marks*.[19] She was aware of the struggles of her father in Northampton and even perceived that he might remove himself if the situation did not improve.[20] Sarah married Elihu Parsons in 1750, and when Jonathan was ejected from his pastorate, the Parsons remained in the Northampton parsonage until 1752 when they joined the family in Stockbridge.[21]

A letter written in the summer of 1741 to Sarah, who was spending time with family in Connecticut, depicts her father in a tenderly compassionate and spiritually involved manner. He writes to stay in touch with her during her absence and encourages her to "improve the great advantage God is thereby putting into your hands for the good of your own soul." Although concerned with her health, his main focus is on the health of her soul: "whatever becomes of [her] body." He commends her to the Lord wishing her "much of the presence of Christ and communion with Him." He concludes by saying he speaks on behalf of the family in sending love to her, encourages her to write often, and commits her to the continual care and mercy of heaven. He signs this letter, "Your loving father."[22] This is certainly a wonderful picture of an affectionate father shepherding his young daughter despite the miles that separate them.

Jerusha Edwards

This 'flower of the family' was believed to partake in Christ's salvation around the time of Whitefield's visit when she was ten.[23] Named after her godly aunt, Jerusha[24] was known for being most like her mother, with a virtuous and godly reputation.[25] Even at the young age of thirteen, her character was praised by Samuel Hopkins who admired her during his time at their home.[26] During Jonathan's attempts to reform the youth of Northampton, Jerusha reported to her father names of boys who skipped their assigned meeting times with their pastor.[27] Like her sisters, Jerusha was able to travel away from home with her father, which she doubtless enjoyed as she grew in faith and understanding of spiritual things.[28] Jerusha is most well known for her servant's heart which is evident in the faithful care of missionary David Brainerd, and her untimely death at the age of seventeen.

Jerusha's faith was displayed as a model to Northampton as her father eulogized her and called for repentance among the young people in the town. Much like his wife Sarah, his daughter Jerusha became a model of true Christian virtue. In the eyes of the town he mourned his daughter's death and yet at the same time trusted it to the providence of God and hoped that this event would become "the beginning of a general awakening and reformation" among the young people in Northampton.[29] That Jerusha embraced the faith of her father is without question, and his impression on her is obvious in her selfless love and service to the Lord through taking care of Brainerd.

Esther Edwards Burr

The life of Esther[30] closely parallels the life of the Edwards family, especially her father. History has benefited greatly from her skills as a diarist, and biographers count on her writings for what is perhaps one of the better resources for understanding the Edwards family specifically and colonial life in general.[31]

Her father Jonathan believed that this precious daughter had come to faith as a result of Whitfield's visit with his family, where he was able to spend specific time with the older girls. Esther fully embraced the godly heritage of her parents. In 1746 she traveled to Long Island with her father in a similar way that her older sister Sarah had.[32] Jonathan frequently involved his children in his affairs and that proved helpful in discipling them in the faith. In the winter of 1746, when Esther was away from home, he would write her to encourage the upkeep of her devotion to Christ. He exhorts her with these words: "God is everywhere, and I hope you will walk closely with him, and have much of his presence." He reminds her that she is daily in the prayers of the family and warmly says, "I am, my dear child, Your affectionate father."[33]

The frontier life of Stockbridge proved to be a love-hate relationship with Esther. At the age of twenty she originally enjoyed life away from Northampton. There was much outdoor activity, and she was friendly with Indian boys as well.[34] In the image of her mother, Esther was frequently engaged in hosting visiting ministers and missionaries at the Stockbridge homestead; this was where she would meet Aaron Burr.[35] They were married in the summer of 1752 in Newark, and because of other travel commitments, only her mother was able to attend.[36] This is far from any reason to assume that her father was not engaged in her life.

Esther enjoyed a blessed life in Newark with her two children, but she also struggled with the reports she received from her extended

[29] Marsden 2003, p. 328

[30] 2/13/1732–4/7/1758 (26 years). Married Rev. Aaron Burr on 6/29/1752 at the age of 20 years old. Her husband died five years later 9/24/1757 when he was 42 years old. Her diary is a very important resource for understanding the life of the Edwards family.

[31] Marsden 2003, p. 403

Fig. 18: Esther Edwards Burr (1732–58)

[32] Marsden 2003, p. 317
[33] Letter no. 71, *WJE* 16:215
[34] Marsden 2003, p. 391
[35] Murray 1987, p. 405
[36] Murray 1987, pp. 379, 405; Marsden 2003, p. 392

[37] Letter no. 165, *WJE* 16:577

[38] Marsden 2003, pp. 423–24

[39] Marsden 2003, p. 425; Murray 1987, p. 419; Winslow 1972, p. 290

[40] Esther writes, "O, I am afraid I shall conduct myself so as to bring dishonor on my God and the religion which I profess! No, rather let me die in this moment, than left to bring dishonor on God's holy name" (Murray, 1987, p. 405).
[41] Marsden 2003, p. 429

[42] Letter no. 231, *WJE* 16:730

family in Stockbridge. In order to ease her concerns, her father would write to her, "'Tis of infinitely more important to have the presence of a heavenly Father, and do make progress towards a heavenly home. Let us all take care that we may meet there at last."[37] Ever more concerned about preparation for eternity than the preservation of this life, he consoles her to look to Christ, but also to take comfort that the family was safe in the good providence of God. Esther would visit her beloved family in the summer of 1756, but she was disappointed to hear that her mother would be away helping Mary with a newborn.[38] Jonathan's relationship with his daughter is seen in a wonderful time of counsel that he was able to share with Esther while she was visiting.[39] She summarized the time spent with her father as a great encouragement, saying that he gave her some specific private and public practices in order to draw herself near to the Lord. One can imagine that Esther missed the times of conversation after dinner growing up, and delighted in the opportunity to share in the wisdom of her beloved father.

It would be to the extended branch of the Edwards family, the Burrs, that tragedy would first strike. Aaron Burr would pass away at the age of forty-two, just five years after marrying Esther. The letters that are available from this time period provide an intimate insight into her struggles, but also testify to a God of sustaining grace. In her grief she confesses that her ultimate concern is that she will conduct herself in such a way that would bring dishonor to God and the religion she professed.[40] She reached out to Jonathan, whom she called her "near and dear affectionate father and guide"[41] in order to confess her grief, but also to speak of how this tragedy had brought her deeper into the realities of the grace and goodness of God. The fact that Esther would react in this way is evidence for how she had been discipled in the past, which would have focused on seeking out the glory of God, and being satisfied to be inside His will no matter the cost. Jonathan wrote to Esther a short two months after losing her husband to encourage her to continue to view this tragedy through sanctified eyes. He exhorts her to fix her eyes upon God: "How good and kind is your heavenly Father!.. Indeed, he is a faithful God; he will remember his covenant forever, and never will fail them that trust in him." Also, he helps to see these events in the larger context of the grace of sanctification: "But I hope, if God should hide his face in some respect, even this will be in faithfulness to you, to purify you, and fit you for yet further and better light."[42]

Jonathan would eventually travel to Newark to be with Esther and so they would be able to share several months of time together. Both he and Esther would take the inoculation for smallpox that would eventually kill them both with Esther following just weeks after him on the seventh of April 1758.

Mary Edwards Dwight

Mary proved to be fiercely loyal to her family throughout her entire life.[43] She was six when Whitefield visited the family, and Edwards would later write that he believed that she came to faith around that time.[44] Concerning her personality as a young lady, even at the age of seven, Samuel Hopkins noticed that she was "beautiful and sprightly."[45] Mary was actively involved in her parents' lives as she proved helpful to her mother in caring for some of her younger siblings, and was also engaged, as her sisters often were, with trips with her father.[46]

Jonathan's relationship with Mary was similar to his other children, very warm and affectionate, but ultimately focused on eternal things. In a letter he wrote to her when she was away from home in the summer of 1749. He speaks seriously about the Lord and encourages her to live for Him. He says, "But my greatest concern is for your soul's good. Though you are at so great a distance from us, yet God is everywhere. You are much out of the reach of our care, but you are every moment in his hands." He commends her to God who is the ultimate Father that can comfort her in ways that her earthly father never could, or desire to. He continues, "I had rather you should remain hundreds of miles distant from us and have God nigh to you by his Spirit than to have you always with us, and live at a distance from God." In order to cultivate this, he implores her to not grow weary in private devotions, and to "meet with God wherever [she] may be, and have much of his divine influences on [her] heart wherever [she] may be." He gives an update on family news, especially concerning the rising issue regarding the sacraments at Northampton. Showing himself to be a loving father and tender shepherd of his daughters' heart, he signs the letter, "your very affectionate father."[47]

When Mary was sixteen she married Timothy Dwight in November 1750, and they lived in Northampton on a plot of land next to the parsonage.[48] The growing Dwight family remained in Northampton even though the rest of the Edwards family moved on to Stockbridge. At various points, her younger siblings would stay with her when the situation on the frontier proved too dangerous.[49] Her mother Sarah also made the sixty-mile trip to help Mary when she had her third child.[50] Living in Northampton was difficult for Mary because she still struggled over what happened to her father at the church. In fact, she still attended regular Lord's Day worship, but would sit in the very back of the foyer where she could be detached from the life of the church, and even made a twelve mile trip to Norwich on communion Sundays rather than partake of the sacrament with the Northampton congregation.[51] Mary is a picture of devotion and loyalty to a man who more than her father, was her pastor as well, and it is clear that she

[43] 4/7/1734–February 1807 (72 years).

[44] Marsden 2003, pp. 207, 214

[45] Marsden 2003, p. 251

[46] Marsden 2003, pp. 322, 363

[47] Letter no. 99, *WJE* 16:288–90

[48] Marsden 2003, p. 363; Murray 1987, p. 370

[49] Marsden 2003, p. 411

[50] Marsden 2003, p. 424

[51] Murray 1987, pp. 353–54; Dodds 1971, p. 155

coveted his spiritual leadership in her life. She would pass away at the age of seventy-two, still a resident of Northampton.

Lucy "Nabby" Edwards Woodbridge

This fifth daughter[52] of the Edwards family was named for Jonathan's sister who had died in the midst of the Great Awakening.[53] In the wake of the colonial revivals, Lucy would have remembered George Whitefield in her home at the age of four.[54] Remembering her as a young woman, her brother Jonathan Jr. said she was a 'beloved and pious woman.'[55] When the family moved to Stockbridge, and the colonies were the backdrop for the war, Lucy, then eighteen years old, went to live with Mary along with younger siblings Pierrepont and Elizabeth.[56] This wasn't for long because the family was close and the separation was for necessity's sake only. A household of so many young women constantly had suitors calling, and in Stockbridge missionary Gideon Hawley expressed his affection for her, calling Lucy 'a charming girl.'[57] Lucy took after her mother and served her family well, including the times her mother had to leave to help other girls in the family take care of newborns.[58] Lucy was especially close with her sister Esther. When Esther visited the family in Stockbridge, Lucy was overcome with joy to see her sister.

Nabby played a significant role in the last year of her father's life. In 1757 she had a scare with smallpox which might have played a part in Edwards' agreement to the inoculation.[59] In 1758 Lucy was with her sister Esther to help care for Sally and Aaron Jr. in Newark. Jonathan was close to Lucy and Esther in the time he was at Princeton because he was living with them. It was to Lucy that Jonathan spoke his last words concerning the 'uncommon union' of him and wife Sarah.[60] Lucy would have watched her father fail in health and eventually pass away under her care. Edwards' final words are the only window we have into what those moments were like, but it can only be assumed that there was much love and affection shared. Lucy would eventually return to Stockbridge to marry Jaheel Woodbridge, with whom she had nine children, passing away in 1786.

Timothy Edwards

The first son of the family and namesake of his grandfather seemed to present Jonathan with much concern. Timothy[61] was two years old when Whitfield visited the family, too young to be counted among the children whom Edwards believed were born again through the means of his friend's visit.[62] Whether the young boy showed prominence in learning, or if his father so desired, Timothy enrolled at the college

[52] 8/31/1738–October 1786 (50 years).

[53] Marsden 2003, p. 172

[54] Marsden 2003, p. 207

[55] Marsden 2003, p. 446

[56] Marsden 2003, p. 411

[57] Marsden 2003, p. 425

[58] Lucy was in charge at the home in Stockbridge when her mother Sarah went to Northampton to assist Mary with the birth of her child (Marsden, 2003, p. 424).

[59] Marsden 2003, p. 493

[60] Marsden 2003, p. 494

[61] 7/25/1738–Autumn 1813 (75 years).

[62] Marsden 2003, p. 207

in New Jersey (later Princeton) at the age of fourteen. He would live with his sister Esther and brother-in-law Aaron Burr while he studied in New Jersey, and his familiarity with his niece Sally and nephew Aaron Jr. might be the reason for his care of them when they became orphaned in 1758.[63]

Jonathan's letters to his son Timothy reflect a very concerned father who is actively involved in the spiritual life of his son. In one letter, written from Stockbridge in 1753, he writes his son who has within the last year left home and is presently struggling with illness at Newark at the Burr home. The central message that he is commending to his son is to seek salvation as a first priority. This is clear with comments such as, "But whether you are sick or well, like to die or like to live, I hope you are earnestly seeking your salvation." He calls him to consider that illness is a mercy of God to make him consider his mortality and seek refuge in Christ for eternal life. Also, rather than seeking the comforts of this world, he advises him to seek the comforts of a heavenly Father: "In God's favor is life, and his loving-kindness is better than life. Whether you are in sickness or health, you infinitely need this." He closes the letter petitioning that God would make his son wise to salvation, and reminding him of the family's love, and signs it "Your affectionate and tender father."[64] One could only imagine the desperate intercession of Edwards as he clearly lacked confidence in the eternal soul of his first-born son.

In another letter from the same year, Edwards attends more to the issues of education, but in a proper context. First, he expresses thanks for apparent healing from illness, but still reminds Timothy to remember his mortality: "Death will certainly come at the time which God has appointed, whether you are prepared or unprepared." However, in the meantime, he encourages his son to make good use of his studies, particular in the use of the original languages. However, he is warned that learning should not be an end in itself, but rather a means to knowing God. Of this Edwards writes, "Above all, I desire that you may have grace to make a good improvement of learning and all other talents, without which they will but aggravate your condemnation." He closes the letter in typical fashion reminding him of the family's love and well wishes, and signs "your tender and affectionate father."[65] The themes of present religious commitment in preparation for eternity are clearly evident in this letter.

In a final letter during Timothy's senior year at the College of New Jersey, Edwards' typical themes are noticeably absent. Instead of speaking on spiritual life and eternity, he writes to offer an account of the family's life at Stockbridge and ask for an account of his life at Princeton. The primary point of interest in this letter is the detailed news about Mary's recent child. The common practice of the Edwards family

[63] Marsden 2003, p. 392; Murray 1987, pp. 437, 446

[64] Letter no. 166, *WJE* 16:578–80

[65] Letter no. 174, *WJE* 16:598–99

in keeping each other up to date on family news certainly suggests that they were a very close family with Jonathan and Sarah at the center keeping it all together through various struggles.[66]

[66] Letter no. 220, *WJE* 16:692–93

Susannah "Sukey" Edwards Porter

Although there isn't as much information about Susannah[67] compared to some of the other children, what we do know is representative of the home she was raised in, and consequently her father as well. She experienced poor health at a very young age and was too young to directly benefit from Whitfield's visit.[68] Susannah was obviously close with her family, especially Esther who she spent time with at Newark in 1755, and was overjoyed when she visited the rest of the family at Stockbridge in 1756.[69]

[67] 6/20/1740–Spring 1802 (61 years).

[68] Marsden 2003, p. 207

[69] Marsden 2003, pp. 410, 423

Sukey's role in the Edwards family intersects two important points in their history. The first is when Jonathan was leaving the family for Princeton. Susannah recalls that he left "as affectionately, as if he should not come again," and as he made his way outside the home he turned and said to his family, "I commit you to God."[70] Such is the picture of a father who loved his family under the knowledge of the God; he trusted his family to the Lord. The second instance where Susannah is notable is after the death of her father. Her mother Sarah wrote what is perhaps the greatest testimony to the role of Jonathan in his family's life. It is clear that he had prepared his family for this moment by helping to form a worldview of life under the sovereignty of God, and therefore not abandoning the godly foundation during this time of struggle. She concludes, saying, "O what a legacy my husband and your father has left us."[71] There could only be speculation as to why Sarah wrote to Susannah; but regardless, this letter is a significant insight into the Edwards family.

[70] Marsden 2003, p. 491; Murray 1987, p. 440

[71] Winslow 1972, p. 319

Eunice Edwards Hunt

Of all the Edwards children Eunice[72] is perhaps the least well known. She was born after her mother's ecstatic experiences in 1742.[73] We know that, like her other sisters, she visited Esther at Princeton. Eunice lived the longest of all her brothers and sisters, passing away in 1822 in North Carolina at the age of 79.[74]

[72] 5/9/1743–Autumn 1822 (79 years).
[73] Marsden 2003, p. 248

[74] Marsden 2003, p. 446

Jonathan Edwards Jr.

It might seem fitting that Jonathan Jr.[75] was the namesake of his father, and the one to follow his steps into the ministry. Jonathan Jr. was just two years old when David Brainerd was living with the Edwards

[75] 5/26/1745–8/1/1801 (56 years). Princeton 1765; M.A. Yale 1769; D.D. Glasgow 1785. New Haven, CT 1769–1795; Colbrook, CT 1796–1799, President of Union College 1799–1801.

family, and although this is very young, perhaps it wasn't too young to make an impression.[76] During 1750 when his father was experiencing the most tension in Northampton, Jonathan Jr. became very sick, which no doubt added to the family pressure.[77] He was comfortable at Stockbridge where, as a six-year-old, he frequently played with Indian boys, but would also later report that he was aware, even as a young man, the financial strains that were on the family.[78] His level of comfort amongst the Indians was due partially to his friends, which were also his schoolmates, a comfort which most likely would have played a role in his decision to serve on the mission field with Gideon Hawley at the age of ten.[79] The fact that Sarah and Jonathan let this young boy journey into Indian Territory as a representative for Christ speaks volumes about their worldview and priorities.

There is a letter that Jonathan wrote his son in 1755 during one of his Indian mission trips with Hawley. Jonathan first speaks of his great love toward his namesake son demonstrated through his great concern and fervent prayers for him. He encourages his son with the reminder that God is everywhere, especially among him at Onohquaga. Jonathan exhorts, "Take heed that you don't forget or neglect [God]." Then in typical fashion, he moves onto the brevity of life, and the motivation to prepare for eternity today. He reports that one of his son's friends, David, which is assumed to be a Mohawk boy, has passed away. Jonathan uses this as an opportunity to remind his son that we do not know the number of our days, and so we should be prepared at any time to meet our Judge. He urges his son, "Never give yourself any rest unless you have good evidence that you are converted and become a new creature." He closes by affirming the family's love and concern for him while he is away from them all, and signs the letter, "Your tender and affectionate father."[80]

As a father, Edwards clearly took great pride in his son's obedience to the Lord's call to the Gospel ministry and the mission field. Jonathan Jr. was thirteen when his father died and it was explained in Edwards' will that his personal library should go to that child which shows interest in the advancement of learning, and Jonathan Jr. received the whole of his father's impressive library.[81] It seems as if he used it well because he would grow to become a formidable intellect much like his father, but interestingly reported that he did not discern that he was converted until after his father's death.[82] The legacy of a father to a son is strong in this connection and is wonderful evidence of the impact Jonathan had on his children, especially his namesake Jonathan Jr.

Elizabeth "Betty" Edwards

Elizabeth,[83] the 'delicate one,' was born just about three months after

[76] Marsden 2003, p. 320

[77] Marsden 2003, p. 363

[78] Marsden 2003, p. 391; Murray 1987, p. 377

[79] Marsden 2003, pp. 399, 404, 412, 421

Fig. 19: Jonathan Edwards, Jr. (1745–1801)

[80] Letter no. 204, *WJE* 16:666–67

[81] Winslow 1972, p. 321

[82] Murray 1987, pp. 446, 452, 454

[83] 5/6/1747–1/1/1762 (14 years).

88 4/8/1750–4/14/1826 (76 years). College of New Jersey 1768; lawyer, politician, public figure.
89 Marsden 2003, p. 363

90 Winslow 1972, p. 320

her sister Jerusha passed away.[84] Like her sister Jerusha, Betty as the family knew her, did not live past her teenage years, dying at the young age of fourteen. She was born just three weeks before David Brainerd came to live with the Edwards family, and because her mother Sarah was attending to this new infant, it gives practical reason why Jerusha would attend to him because she was the first available and most eligible nurse for Brainerd.[85] When the family was living at Stockbridge, Elizabeth would live with Mary in Northampton for a span of time when it was not safe to live on the frontier during the wars.[86] Elizabeth would eventually return to Northampton at the age of eleven with her sister Mary when her mother died in 1758.[87] It is clear that the family lived to take care of one another even after their parents passed from this world, which is a testimony to the home that they were first raised in.

Pierrepont "Pinty" Edwards

Like his sister Eunice, there seems to be much less information about the youngest son of the Edwards family.[88] He was born just three months before his father was officially put out of his pulpit in Northampton.[89] Pierrepont would have only known life at Stockbridge, and even though he was only seven when his father died, there can be no doubt he was left with a significant impression of him.[90] The hours spent in the small close study on the frontier modeled a life of piety before Pinty, and there could be no doubt that it affected him the same way it did his brothers and sisters. Like his brothers, he entered the College of New Jersey, where he graduated in 1768.

Jonathan Edwards the Father

By tracing the history of Edwards through the lives of his children, we are able to understand a more complete and intimate image of this towering figure. There is abundant evidence to conclude that he was much more of a family man than the infamous *thirteen hours* might suggest. The legacy of Jonathan Edwards is more than the voluminous works of philosophy and theology; it is also the covenant blessing and spiritual legacy of children of God shepherded to love the Lord from a young age and walk with Him throughout their lives.

Edwards was entirely consistent in how he led his family. The two steady and enduring themes are: first, the importance of present religious commitment, and second, the brevity of life and therefore the necessity to prepare for eternity. To the very end of his life, his heart was for his family, to which he spoke these final words to Lucy, "Trust in God, and you need not fear."[91] The focus of his life and parenting was the Almighty. He was constantly pointing his children past himself toward God. Speaking of his children in general at the time of his death he said, "And as to my children, you are now like to be left fatherless, which I hope will be an inducement to you all to seek a Father, who will never fail you."[92]

Edwards wanted his children to share in the love and hunger that their father had for God. In a letter to young Jonathan Jr. he exhorts his son:

> Always set God before your eyes, and live in his fear, and seek him every day with all diligence: for 'tis he, and he only can make you happy or miserable, as he pleases; and your life and health, and the eternal salvation of your soul, and your all in this life and that which is to come, depends on his will and pleasure.[93]

It can easily be seen that his life left a lasting impression upon his children who mourned his passing. In a letter to Esther, Sarah reflects on the loss of her beloved husband and reminds her children, "Oh what a legacy my husband, and your father, has left us! We are all given to God: and there I am, and love to be."[94] In considering the life and legacy of Jonathan Edwards, what better evidence could there be for his tender affection for his family than the living breathing testimonies of those he loved most.

[92] Marsden 2003, p. 494

[93] Letter no. 204, *WJE* 16:667

[94] Marsden 2003, p. 495

Bibliography

Christopher Atwood. *Jonathan Edwards's Doctrine of Justification: A New Reading of Edwards's Treatises, Sermons, and Miscellanies*. PhD thesis, Wheaton College, 2014.

Joel R. Beeke. *The Quest for Full Assurance: The Legacy of Calvin and His Successors*. Banner of Truth Trust, Edinburgh, 1999.

Rhys S. Bezzant. *Jonathan Edwards and the Church*. Oxford University Press, New York, 2014.

James Montgomery Boice and Philip Graham Ryken. *The Doctrines of Grace*. Crossway, Wheaton, IL, 2002.

Robert L. Boss. *God-Haunted World: The Elemental Theology of Jonathan Edwards*. Privately Published, Fort Worth, TX, 2015.

Paul Brewster. *Andrew Fuller: Model Pastor-Theologian*. B&H Academic, Nashville, 2010.

S. Pearce Carey. *Samuel Pearce, A.A.: The Baptist Brainerd*. Carey Press, London, 1913.

Bryan Chapell. *Christ-Centered Preaching*. Baker Books, Grand Rapids, 1994.

Conrad Cherry. *The Theology of Jonathan Edwards: A Reappraisal*. Indiana University Press, Bloomington, 1990.

Chris Chun. Sense of the Heart: Jonathan Edwards' Legacy in the Writings of Andrew Fuller. *Eusebia*, IX, 2008.

Samuel Clarke. *Remarks upon a Book Entituled, A Philosophical Enquiry Concerning Human Liberty*. London, 1717.

Anthony Collins. *A Philosophical Inquiry Concerning Human Liberty, 2nd ed., corrected*. London, 1717.

Joseph A. Conforti. *Jonathan Edwards, Religious Tradition, and American Culture*. University of North Carolina Press, Chapel Hill, NC, 1995.

Oliver Crisp. *Retrieving Doctrine: Essays in Reformed Theology*. Intervarsity Press, Downers Grove, IL, 2010.

Oliver Crisp. *Jonathan Edwards on God and Creation*. Oxford University Press, Oxford, 2012.

Oliver Crisp. *Deviant Calvinism: Broadening the Reformed Tradition*. Fortress Press, Minneapolis, MN, 2014.

Oliver Crisp. *Jonathan Edwards among the Theologians*. Eerdmans, Grand Rapids, MI, 2015.

Elisabeth D. Dodds. *Marriage to a Difficult Man: The Uncommon Union of Jonathan & Sarah Edwards*. Banner of Truth Trust, Edinburgh, 1971.

Jonathan Edwards. *Freedom of the Will*, volume 1 of *The Works of Jonathan Edwards*. Yale University Press, New Haven, 1957.

Jonathan Edwards. *Religious Affections*, volume 2 of *The Works of Jonathan Edwards*. Yale University Press, New Haven, 1959.

Jonathan Edwards. *Original Sin*, volume 3 of *The Works of Jonathan Edwards*. Yale University Press, New Haven, 1970.

Jonathan Edwards. *The Great Awakening*, volume 4 of *The Works of Jonathan Edwards*. Yale University Press, New Haven, 1972.

Jonathan Edwards. *Scientific and Philosophical Writings*, volume 6 of *The Works of Jonathan Edwards*. Yale University Press, New Haven, 1980.

Jonathan Edwards. *The Life of David Brainerd*, volume 7 of *The Works of Jonathan Edwards*. Yale University Press, New Haven, 1985.

Jonathan Edwards. *Ethical Writings*, volume 8 of *The Works of Jonathan Edwards*. Yale University Press, New Haven, 1989a.

Jonathan Edwards. *A History of the Work of Redemption*, volume 9 of *The Works of Jonathan Edwards*. Yale University Press, New Haven, 1989b.

Jonathan Edwards. *Sermons and Discourses, 1720–1723*, volume 10 of *The Works of Jonathan Edwards*. Yale University Press, New Haven, 1992.

Jonathan Edwards. *Typological Writings*, volume 11 of *The Works of Jonathan Edwards*. Yale University Press, New Haven, 1993.

Jonathan Edwards. *The Miscellanies, a–500*, volume 13 of *The Works of Jonathan Edwards*. Yale University Press, New Haven, 1994.

Jonathan Edwards. *Sermons and Discourses, 1723–1729*, volume 14 of *The Works of Jonathan Edwards*. Yale University Press, New Haven, 1997.

Jonathan Edwards. *Letters and Personal Writings*, volume 16 of *The Works of Jonathan Edwards*. Yale University Press, New Haven, 1998.

Jonathan Edwards. *Sermons and Discourses, 1730–1733*, volume 17 of *The Works of Jonathan Edwards*. Yale University Press, New Haven, 1999.

Jonathan Edwards. *The "Miscellanies" 501–832*, volume 18 of *The Works of Jonathan Edwards*. Yale University Press, New Haven, 2000.

Jonathan Edwards. *Sermons and Discourses, 1734–1738*, volume 19 of *The Works of Jonathan Edwards*. Yale University Press, New Haven, 2001.

Jonathan Edwards. *Writings on the Trinity, Grace, and Faith*, volume 21 of *The Works of Jonathan Edwards*. Yale University Press, New Haven, 2002.

Jonathan Edwards. *Sermons and Discourses, 1739–1742*, volume 22 of *The Works of Jonathan Edwards*. Yale University Press, New Haven, 2003.

Jonathan Edwards. *The "Miscellanies" 1153–1360*, volume 23 of *The Works of Jonathan Edwards*. Yale University Press, New Haven, 2004.

Jonathan Edwards. *Sermons and Discourses, 1743–1758*, volume 25 of *The Works of Jonathan Edwards*. Yale University Press, New Haven, 2006.

Jonathan Edwards. *Sermons, Series II, 1729–1731*, volume 45 of *The Works of Jonathan Edwards Online*. Jonathan Edwards Center at Yale University, http://edwards.yale.edu, 2008a.

Jonathan Edwards. *Sermons, Series II, 1737*, volume 52 of *The Works of Jonathan Edwards Online*. Jonathan Edwards Center at Yale University, http://edwards.yale.edu, 2008b.

Jonathan Edwards. *Sermons, Series II, 1739*, volume 54 of *The Works of Jonathan Edwards Online*. Jonathan Edwards Center at Yale University, http://edwards.yale.edu, 2008c.

Sinclair Ferguson, David F. Wright, and J.I. Packer, editors. *New Dictionary of Theology*. Intervarsity Press, Downers Grove, IL, 1998.

Norman S. Fiering. Benjamin Franklin and the Way to Virtue. *American Quarterly*, 30, Summer 1978.

Norman S. Fiering. *Jonathan Edwards's Moral Thought and Its British Context*. University of North Carolina Press, Chapel Hill, 1981.

Andrew Fuller. *The Complete Works of the Rev. Andrew Fuller*. Sprinkle Publications, Harrisonburg, VA, 1988.

John H. Gerstner. *The Rational Biblical Theology of Jonathan Edwards*. Ligonier Ministries, Orlando, FL, 1991-93.

Graeme Goldsworthy. *According to Plan: The Unfolding Revelation of God in the Bible*. Eerdmans, Grand Rapids, MI, 1991.

Justo L. González. *Mañana: Christian Theology from a Hispanic Perspective*. Abingdon Press, Nashville, TN, 1990.

Sidney Greidanus. *Preaching Christ from the Old Testament: A Contemporary Hermeneutical Model*. Eerdmans, Grand Rapids, MI, 1999.

Collin Hansen. *Young, Restless, Reformed: A Journalist's Journey with the New Calvinists*. Crossway, Wheaton, IL, 2008.

Joseph G. Haroutunian. Jonathan Edwards: Theologian of the Great Commandment. *Theology Today*, 1, 1944.

Michael A.G. Haykin. Writing the Life of Samuel Pearce: Andrew Fuller's Edwardean Biography. Southern Baptist Theological Seminary class notes.

Michael A.G. Haykin, editor. *The Armies of the Lamb: The Spirituality of Andrew Fuller*. Joshua Press, Dundas, Ontario, 2001.

Paul Helm, editor. *Treatise on Grace and Other Posthumous Writings Including Observations on the Trinity*. James Clarke, London, 1971.

Edward Herbert. *De Veritate*. J.W. Arrowsmith, Ltd., Bristol, 1937.

Thomas Hobbes. *Of Libertie and Necessitie: A Treatise wherein All Controversie Concerning Predesination, Election, Free-will, Grace, Merits, Reprobation, Etc. Is Fully Decided and Cleared in Answer to a Treatise Written by the Bishop of London-derry, on the Same Subject.* W.B. for F. Eaglesfield, London, 1654.

Thomas Hobbes. *The Questions Concerning Liberty, Necessity, and Chance. Clearly Stated and Debated between D. Bramhall Bishop of Derry, and Thomas Hobbes of Malmesbury.* Andrew Crook, London, 1656.

Thomas Hobbes and John Bramhall. *Hobbes and Bramhall on Liberty and Necessity*. Cambridge University Press, Cambridge, 1999.

Charles Hodge. *Systematic Theology*. James Clarke, London, 1960.

Stephen Holmes. *God of Grace & God of Glory*. Eerdmans, Grand Rapids, MI, 2000.

Samuel Hopkins. *The Life and character of the late Reverend Jonathan Edwards, President of the College of New Jersey*. S. Kneeland, Boston, 1765.

Hans Hut. *Early Anabaptist Spirituality*, chapter The Mystery of Baptism. Paulist Press, New Jersey, 1994.

Robert Jenson. *America's Theologian: A Recommendation of Jonathan Edwards*. Oxford University Press, New York, 1988.

William H. Kimnach, Kenneth P. Minkema, and Douglas A. Sweeney, editors. *The Sermons of Jonathan Edwards: A Reader*. Yale University Press, New Haven, 1999.

B.K. Kuiper. *The Church in History*. Eerdmans, Grand Rapids, 1951.

Steven Lawson. *The Unwavering Resolve of Jonathan Edwards*. Reformation Trust, Lake Mary, FL, 2008.

Sang Hyun Lee and Allen C. Guelzo, editors. *Edwards in Our Time: Jonathan Edwards and the Shaping of American Religion*. Eerdmans, Grand Rapids, 1999.

James C. Livingston. *Modern Christian Thought, 2nd ed.*, chapter The Religion of Reason. Fortress Press, Minneapolis, MN, 2006.

D. Martyn Lloyd-Jones. *The Puritans: Their Origins and Successors*. Banner of Truth Trust, Edinburgh, 1987.

Russell Re Manning. *The Oxford Handbook of Natural Theology*. Oxford University Press, Oxford, 2013.

Jonathan S. Marko. Revisiting the Question: Is Anthony Collins the Author of the 1729 Dissertation on Liberty and Necessity? *Philosophy and Theology*, 22(1 & 2), 2010a.

Jonathan S. Marko. Free Choice in Calvin's Concepts of Regeneration and Moral Agency: How Free Are We? *Ashland Theological Journal*, 42, 2010b.

Jonathan S. Marko. *Re-visioning Reason, Revelation, and Rejection in John Locke's An Essay Concerning Human Understanding and John Toland's Christianity Not Mysterious*. PhD thesis, Calvin Theological Seminary, 2012.

Jonathan S. Marko. The Promulgation of Right Morals: John Locke on the Church and the Christian as the Salvation of Society. *Journal of Markets and Morality*, 19(1), 2016.

George Marsden. *Jonathan Edwards: A Life*. Yale University Press, New Haven, 2003.

Michael J. McClymond. *Encounters with God: An Approach to the Theology of Jonathan Edwards*. Oxford University Press, New York, 1998.

Michael J. McClymond and Gerald R. McDermott. *The Theology of Jonathan Edwards*. Oxford University Press, New York, 2012.

Gerald R. McDermott. *The Princeton Companion to Jonathan edwards*, chapter Missions and Native Americans. Princeton University Press, Princeton, 1995.

Alister E. McGrath. *Re-Imagining Nature: The Promise of a Christian Natural Theology*. Wiley-Blackwell, West Sussex, UK, 2016.

Herman Melville. *Moby-Dick*. W.W. Norton & Company, New York, 2002.

Perry Miller. *Jonathan Edwards*. Univesity of Nebraska Press, Lincoln, NE, 2005.

Josh Moody. *The God-Centered Life: Insights fro Jonathan Edwards for Today*. Regent College Publishing, New York, 2007.

Josh Moody, editor. *Jonathan Edwards and Justification*. Crossway, Wheaton, IL, 2012.

J.P. Moreland and William Lane Craig. *Philosophical Foundations for a Christian Worldview*. IVP Academic, Downers Grove, IL, 2003.

Richard A. Muller. *Dictionary of Latin and Greek Theological Terms: Drawn Principally from Protestant Scholastic Theology*. Baker Book House, Grand Rapids, 1985.

Richard A. Muller. The Dogmatic Function of St. Thomas' 'Proofs': A Protestant Appreciation. *Fides et Historia*, 5(24), 1992.

Richard A. Muller. *The Grace of God, the Bondage of the Will, Vol. 2: Historical and Theological Perspectives on Calvinism*, chapter Grace, Election, and Contingent Choice: Arminius' Gambit and the Reformed Response. Baker Books, Grand Rapids, MI, 1995.

David Murray. *Jesus on Every Page: 10 Simple Ways to Seek and Find Christ in the Old Testament*. Thomas Nelson, Nashville, TN, 2013.

Iain Murray. *Jonathan Edwards: A New Biography*. Banner of Truth Trust, 1987.

Iain H. Murray. Thomas Hooker and the Doctrine of Conversion: The Way to Christ: Part 4. *Banner of Truth Magazine*, 199, April 1980.

Tom Nettles. The Influence of Jonathan Edwards on Andrew Fuller. *Eusebia*, IX, 2008.

J.I. Packer. *A Quest for Godliness: The Puritan Vision of the Christian Life.* Crossway Books, Wheaton, IL, 2010.

Werner Packull. In Search of the 'Common Man' in Early German Anabaptist Ideology. *The Sixteenth Century Journal*, 17(1), 1986.

Earnest A. Payne. *The First Generation: Early Leaders of the Baptist Missionary Society in England and America.* Carey Press, London, 1936.

Michael Peterson et al. *Reason and Religious Belief: An Introduction to the Philosophy of Religion*, 5th ed., chapter Divine Action: How Does God Relate to the World. Oxford University Press, Oxford, 2013.

John Piper. *God's Passion for His Glory.* Crossway, Wheaton, IL, 1998.

Noel Piper. *A God Entranced Vision of All Things: The Legacy of Jonathan Edwards*, chapter Sarah Edwards: Jonathan Edwards's Home and Haven. Crossway Books, Wheaton, IL, 2004.

Jeremy Pittsley. Andrew Fuller and Particular Redemption. *Eusebia*, IX, 2008.

John Herman Randall Jr. *The Making of the Modern Mind.* Columbia University Press, New York, 1976.

Gordon Rupp. Thomas Müntzer, Hans Huth and the Gospel of all Creatures. *Bulletin of the John Rylands Library*, 43(2), 1961.

Susan E. Schreiner. *The Theater of His Glory: Nature and the Natural Order in the Thought of John Calvin.* Labyrinth Press, Durham, 1983.

John E. Smith. *Jonathan Edwards: Puritan, Preacher, Philosopher.* University of Notre Dame Press, Notre Dame, 1992.

John E. Smith, Harry S. Stout, and Kenneth P. Minkema, editors. *A Jonathan Edwards Reader.* Yale University Press, New Haven, 2005.

R.C. Sproul. *The Freedom of the Will.* Soli Deo Gloria, Morgan, PA, 1996.

Leslie Stephen. *History of English Thought in the Eighteenth Century*, 3rd ed. Harbinger, London, 1962.

Leo Strauss. *Persecution and the Art of Writing.* University of Chicago Press, Chicago, 1952.

Leo Strauss. *Natural Right and History*. University of Chicago Press, Chicago, 1953.

Kyle Strobel. *Jonathan Edwards's Theology: A Reinterpretation*. Bloomsbury T&T Clark, New York, 2014.

Robert E. Sullivan. *John Toland and the Deist Controversy: A Study in Adaptations*. Harvard University Press, Cambridge, 1982.

G. Tanzella-Nitti. The Two Books Prior to the Scientific Revolution. *Perspectives on Science and Christian Faith*, 57(3), 2005.

Henry David Thoreau. *Walden*. Borders Classics, Ann Arbor, 2006.

Matthew Tindal. *Christianity as Old as the Creation: or, The Gospel, a Republication of the Religion of Nature*. London, 1730.

Francis Turretin. *Institutes of Elenctic Theology*. P&R Publishing, Phillipsburg, 1992.

Stephen Williams. *An Account of the Growth of Deism in England*. London, 1696.

E.O. Wilson. *The Creation: An Appeal to Save Life on Earth*. W.W. Norton & Company, New York, 2006.

Ola Elizabeth Winslow. *Jonathan Edwards, 1703–1758: A Biography*. Octagon Books, New York, 1972.

Maarten Wisse. Habitus fidei: an essay on the history of a concept. *Scottish Journal of Theology*, 56(2), 2003.

Index